A WINTER DIARY
AND OTHER POEMS

BY MARK VAN DOREN

SPRING THUNDER

7 P.M.

NOW THE SKY

JONATHAN GENTRY

A WINTER DIARY

And Other Poems

BY MARK VAN DOREN

New York
THE MACMILLAN COMPANY
1935

Set up and printed.
Published January, 1935.

PRINTED IN THE UNITED STATES OF AMERICA
BY THE STRATFORD PRESS, INC., NEW YORK

Certain of these poems appeared first in The American Poetry Journal, The American Review, Blues, The Bookman, Books (The New York Herald Tribune), The Brooklyn Daily Eagle, The Columbia Review, Contempo, Harper's Magazine, The Nation, The New Republic, The New Yorker, Palms, and The Saturday Review of Literature.

CONTENTS

A WINTER DIARY

A Winter Diary

This was not written then, when measuring time
Ran smoothly to unalterable rhyme;
When even song—but still it is unsounded—
Kept the pure tally that has been confounded.
This was not written then, when sudden spring
Not yet had threatened winter, and no thing
Stood colder than the skin of apple trees.
Now every top is bursting into bees;
Now all of them, solidified to light,
Reflect a cloudy fire, as high, as white
As any sky in summer; and at last
Sharp edges of a shadow have been cast.
Thus sudden spring, with sudden summer near,
Has made a certain winter disappear—
The winter of all winters I would keep
Had I the power to put this warmth asleep
And make the world remember what I saw.
But who has power against a season's law?
Who lives a winter over, who is proof
Against the rain of months upon his roof?
A certain winter fades that I had thought
Forever in live colors to have caught.
A certain moveless winter more than moves—
Runs backward, and oblivion's great grooves
Lie deeper in the distance, and tomorrow
Nothing will be there save mist and sorrow.
Therefore must I fix it while I may—
Feign records, and upon this single day
Tie months of time together, in pretended
Sequence till they once again are ended.

* * * So it is autumn, when the city reaches,
Pulling us home from mountains and from beaches;
Down the curved roads and from the crescent sands
To oblong streets among divided lands.
Yet not us four. It is the year we stay
And watch the town-returners pour away.
Now the last stragglers of the stream have gone;
Here now we stand upon a thinning lawn—
The shade wind-shattered, and the cut grass sleeping—
Here then we stand and to the country's keeping
Tender four faces. Not a leaf that falls
But flutters through a memory of walls—
Flutters, with more to follow, till they weave
This solitude we shall at last believe.

* * * October sunshine, and a summer's day!
Yet not the heaviness long wont to lay
Slow skies upon our heads and bind us round
With the full growth of a too fruitful ground.
The morning sun was southerly, and noon
Came swiftly, and the day was over soon:
An airy thing time tossed us for our pleasure,
Blue, and wide-blown, and rich with gold leaf-treasure.
The solid green is gone, the trees are fire—
Cool fire, and top-contained, without desire;
Not caring if it lives, for lo, all day
Wind bullied it and bore the sparks away.
October sunshine and red-ember drifts;
So the long burden of a summer lifts.

* * * November rain all night, the last of three
Dark nights and mornings. We have been to see

The brook that piles grey water down the meadows.
Grey water, and there is no sun for shadows;
No wind for bare tree-talk, no thing but spreading
Rain; no thing but rain, wherein the treading
Crow-feet leave thin tracks, and grass is drowned
With a contented and a final sound.
Safely indoors now, with a fire to dry us,
We hear a whole long year go slipping by us—
Backward to die, with nothing left ahead
Save solitude and silence, and a thread
Of days that will conduct us through the cold.
The window-panes are waterfalls that fold
Small misty visions of our valley's end.
The rain is sewing curtains that will rend
And rise another day; but shut us now
In such a world as mice have up the mow.
Thus do we know ourselves at last alone—
And laugh at both the kittens, who have grown
Till here they lie, prim figures by the fire,
Paws folded, aping age and undesire.
The boys would have them up again to play.
But they are sudden-old; it is the day
For dreaming of enclosure, and of being
All of the world time missed as he was fleeing.
They think, the furry fools, to live forever.
So then do we—the curtains lifted never.

* * * It is December, and the setting sun
Drops altogether leftward of the one
Long mountain-back we used to measure by.
The maple limbs swing upward, grey and dry,
And print the lawn—now naked for the snow—

With lines that might be nothing. But we know.
We see them there across the bitten ground,
Dark lace upon the iron, and catch the sound
Of half a world contracting under cold.
Slowly it shrinks, for it is wise and old,
And waits; and in its wisdom will be spared.
So is the frosted garden-plot prepared.
The withered tops, arustle row by row,
Fear nothing still to come; for all must go.
That is their wisdom, as it is the horse's—
Whose coat the wind already reinforces,
There in the blowing paddock past the gate.
The four of us a long day, working late,
Confined her where she grazes, building the fence
She leans on; yet she would not wander hence.
She drops her head and nibbles the brown grass,
Unmindful of a season that will pass;
Long-coated, with a rump the wind can ruffle;
Shoeless, and free; but soon the snow will muffle
All of her four black feet, that study a line
Down to the ponies' corner under the pine.
So have the field-mice, folding their startled ears,
Burrowed away from owls and flying fears.
So have the hunters ceased upon the hills;
The last shot echoes and the woodland stills;
And here, along the house, the final flower
Lets fall its rusty petals hour by hour.

* * * So, in December, we ourselves stand ready.
The season we have dared is strong and heady,
But there is many a weapon we can trust.
Five cellar shelves that were but layered dust

Are wiped to kitchen neatness, and confine
Clear jellies that will soothe us when we dine:
Crab-apple, quince, and hardly-ripened grape,
With jam from every berry, and the shape
Of cherries showing pressed against the jar;
Whole pears; and where the tall half-gallons are,
Tomatoes with their golden seeds; and blunt
Cucumbers that the early ground-worms hunt.
The highest shelf, beneath the spidery floor,
Holds pumpkins in a row, with squash before—
Dark, horny Hubbards that will slice in half
And come with pools of butter as we laugh,
Remembering the frost that laid the vines
Like blackened string—September's valentines.
Firm corn, and tapering carrots, and the blood
Of beets complete the tally of saved food;
Yet over in a corner, white and square,
Is the big bin with our potato-share.
Then seven barrels of apples standing by.
We brought them down the ladder when a high
Stiff wind was there to whip us, hand and cheek;
And wheeled them to the barn, where many a week
They filled the tightest chamber; but they found
More certain safety here below the ground—
The Baldwins to be eaten, and the Spies;
But Greenings are for betty and for pies.
A dusty cellar window, old as stone,
Lets in grey light—a slowly spreading cone
Sharp-ended here, and shining, at the shelves.
All of the other spaces wrapped themselves
In darkness long ago; and there the wood
Remembers a great sky wherein they stood—

The twenty trees I walked with Louis, marking,
Once in a mist of rain; then axes barking
Through the wet, chilly weeks, with ring of wedges
Under the blows of iron alternate sledges—
Louis's and Laurier's, of equal skill.
These were the two woodchoppers whom the still
Small faces of the boys watched day by day.
They sat among brown leaves, so far away
We barely could hear their shouting as the saw
Paused, and the great trunk trembled, and a raw
Circle of odorous wood gaped suddenly there.
Now maple and oak and cherry, and a rare
Hard chestnut piece, with hickory and birch,
Piled here in shortened lengths, await my search—
Coming with lantern and with leather gloves
To choose what provender the furnace loves.
From wall to wall a dozen resting rows:
We shall be warm, whatever winter blows.
So for the range upstairs a mound uprises,
By the back fence, of birch in sapling sizes.
Old Bailey cut them through a lonely fall—
He and his axe together, that was all:
They in a thicket, and the white poles gleaming;
Now a high frozen pile the sun is steaming.
We shall be warm, whatever north wind catches
Any of us outside the rattling latches;
Down the sloped road, or where the yard descends
To the barn's angle with its gusty ends,
Or higher, beyond the garden and the orchard—
We shall not be snow-worried or wind-tortured.
The armor we have sent for has arrived.
The great book spread its pages, and we dived

Like cormorants for prey among the rocks;
And chose, and duly ordered—and the box
Came yesterday. A winter's woolen wraps:
Thick-wristed mittens and two stocking caps;
Three fleece-lined jackets that will turn all weather,
And one cut neat for ladies out of leather;
Red sweaters, nut-brown shirts, and rubber-soled
Great workman's shoes for wading in the cold.
We shall be warm—or we can stamp indoors,
Wool failing, till the supper and the chores.

* * * So quietly it came that we could doubt it.
There was no wind from anywhere to shout it.
Simply it came, the inescapable cold,
Sliding along some world already old
And stretched already there had we perceived it.
Now by this hour the least one has believed it.
Snippy, the lesser kitten, lies entangled
Deep in the fur of Snappy, where a dangled
Feed-sack drapes a box inside the shed.
I found them with the lantern, playing dead—
Those very creatures, Snippy and her brother,
Who in the orange sunset tumbled each other,
Lithe by the stepping-stone. Through such a night
How often have they put the frost to flight;
How often, when the blackness made them bolder,
Have they confounded time, that grew no colder.
Yet not this night; they recognize the god,
As in the barn the black mare, left to nod,
Stands in her blanket, dozing. I have come
From tending her, and heard the ominous hum
Of branches that no wind moved overhead;

Only a tightness and a stealth instead.
The stiffened world turns hard upon its axis,
Laboring; but these yellow lamps relax us,
Here in the living-room at either end.
She by the south one, I by the north pretend
Forgetfulness of pavements; or remark
How very dead the sky is, and how dark—
In passing, with the air of two that pore
On things familiar, having been before.
It is our way of knowing what is near.
This is the time, this is the holy year
We planned for, casting every cable off.
That was a board-creak; that was the horse's cough;
That was no wind, we say; and looking down,
Smile at the wolf-dog, Sam, who dreams of brown
Clipped fields that he will lope in when he wakes.
He dreams, and draws his ankles up, and slakes
Imaginary thirsts at frozen pools.
He is the wolf-dog, he is the one that fools
New comers up the yard; for gentler beast
Prowled never to the pantry for a feast.
He is the boys' companion, who at dusk
Ran rings with them tonight, and worried the husk
Of daylight in his teeth, and stood his hair
Wind-upright. Now he sleeps unthinking there,
Companion of the boys, who long ago
Climbed the dark stairs to bed. So we below
Should come there too, we say; and say it again,
And laugh to hear the clock tick out the ten.
We are not sleepy; this is the holy year.
Let it tick on to midnight, and for cheer

Start coffee in the kitchen, while I spread
Bright jam upon the goodness of cut bread.

* * * We were awakened by a double shout:
"Get up, you lazy people, and look out!"
There was a weight of stillness on my eyes—
But in my ears innumerable sighs
Of snowflakes settling groundward past the glass.
I stood and stared, saying for jest "Alas!
My sight fails, I can see the merest dim
Milk-whiteness!" "We must bring it up to him!"
Cried one; and both were going, when I told them:
"Dress!" So now, as breakfast waits, behold them
Marching through a mist of falling specks.
They stop and raise their faces, and it flecks
Their foreheads till they laugh; then treading on,
Leave tracks across the swiftly thickening lawn.
I let them go this morning for the milk—
The car wheels turning softly in a silk
New coverlet as wide as eyes could see.
The chimney smoke was rising, round and free,
From every ridge of shingles—even there
Where Grandmother waved and pointed at the air.
The wolf-dog running with us need not pause,
Tasting the untamed whiteness; for his jaws
Dipped as he loped along, and fiercely entered
Now the far past wherein his mind was centered.
Back at the barn the Shetland ponies wheeled,
Biting each other's manes, their little field
Grown boundless by some fantasy, and fenceless.
They romped like shaggy dogs, and were as senseless,

Fluttering at the gate, as moths, and small.
They waited for the big one in the stall.
She whinnied as we came, and only stopped
When I rose up the ladder and hay dropped.
She will have finished breakfast in an hour.
So we, and through a sudden whirling shower
Shall bring her to the ponies. Then our talk
Will come once more to sleds, and up the walk
I shall again make promises—and keep them,
Thinking of flakes and how a wind can heap them.
This wind is gentle, and the grey sheet sways.
I am no prophet if it falls and stays.

* * * All yesterday it melted, and at night
Was nothing, and the prophecy was right.
But in a play-house corner stand the sleds—
Almost as high as the excited heads
Of two that will be on them when the slopes
Glisten once more. And so the boys have hopes
While I have present pleasure; for the ground
Grows musical wherever I am bound.
The mud was gone as quickly as the snow:
An afternoon of thaw, but then a low
Crisp sunset sound of shrinking, and the crack
Of coldness like a panther coming back.
Tonight the snowless evening and the moon
Kept my late feet contented with a tune
More ancient than the meadows, where the stones
Rise ever up—unburiable bones.
The bareness of the world was like a bell
My feet, accustomed, struck; and striking well,
Let the rung sound be mingled with the dry

Primeval winter moonlight flowing by.
Alone outdoors and late, the resonant lawn
Moved with me as I lagged, and moving on
Bore all my senses fieldward to those bones
Of permanence, the unalterable stones.
There is no such intensity of lasting
Anywhere out of meadows, where the fasting
Grasses worship something in December
Older than any moist root can remember;
Older than age, drier than any drouth;
Something not to be praised by word of mouth.
I did not praise them then, nor shall henceforth;
But shall remind me, so, what change is worth—
Timothy round a rock, and daisies hiding
Something that will be there again—abiding
Longer than hope and stronger than old despair;
Something not to be dated under the air.
I looked at stones; and faces looked at me:
Sidewise, always sidewise, past a tree
Or slanting down some corner, or obliquely
Squinting where the moon fell, and as weakly.
I saw them not but knew them—the tired faces
Of those who may not leave their acred places:
Those of a time long gone that never dies.
You know it by the darkness of their eyes,
And by the way they work to comprehend
Who lives here now beyond a century's end.
Who lives and does not labor, and makes light
Of the grim gods that once were day, were night;
That carved a cheek, bent breasts, and knotted hands.
Not one of them withdraws or understands.
Not one of them but looked at me; and I,

Intruder here, seemed helpless to reply.
Not by their older choosing are we here,
Not by their doom made free of gods and fear.
Was then the better time? I said—and thought
How excellently winter moonshine taught
The shapes of winter trees. That maple there,
How shadeless, how upflowing, and how fair!
Even without their leaves the elm-limbs drooped;
The alders leaned; and birches interlooped
Their lacy, blackened fingers past the pines.
The great dead chestnut where the loud crow dines
Writhed on, its mighty arms unskilled to fall.
The evergreens were solid over all,
And hickories and tulips, few of limb,
Held what they had straight out for time to trim.
Was then the better world, I wondered—daring
Suddenly now an answer from the staring
People of old days, the accusing faces.
But none of us, tree-watching on these places,
Ever will hear a sentence from the source.
Gone is their blood, and spent their bitter force;
They only live to chafe us down the wind
And leave us ever afterward thin-skinned:
Wondering on them, the only-good,
On whom these lighter feet too long intrude.

* * * We have had company of Friday nights.
We have looked out of windows till the lights
Of cars too long in coming dipped and streamed;
Then ended by the door as time had dreamed.
Two late ones from the city, blinking here
In the warm lamplight, with the kittens near—

These have been shown their room, the spare northeast one;
Have laughed and begged a bite: even the least one,
Even a crust to pay them for the ride.
Already coffee bubbled, fit to glide,
As quickly as cups were ready, from the spout.
Already there were cookies placed about;
And soon the supper entered that would keep us
Longer awake than wise, with talk to steep us
In every winter's moment we had missed.
So we unrolled our pleasures, till the list
Grew endless, and the meaning of it fled.
So, as the boys before us, up to bed.
For all of us a lazy breakfast waited,
With coffee and tobacco, brownly mated,
Warming the day to come. We tilted chairs,
Lit pipes, and fingered forks; till unawares
Time bore us half to noon; and looking out,
We argued what the weather was about.
Some said it would be overcast till night,
Settling themselves forever; but the right
Was mostly with the walkers and the curious.
First then the barn, where the black mare was furious,
Tossing as I excused our long delay.
No answer, but the eyes among the hay
Dived languorously and said I was forgiven.
The cutter by the car could not be driven.
I found it years ago and dragged it here
To a dry floor and braced it; but the clear
Curved figure will be never swift again.
Snow or no snow, it is for living men
Another last reminder of the old
Dim people who are dead. A crimson fold

Of lining flaps and braves the window frost.
But all the rest is poor and language-lost:
No bells to shake, no orders to be going
Down a long hill where only time is snowing—
Flake by flake forgotten, till the white
Far past of it is shadowy with night.
We took the road and turned, and crossed the bridge;
Then—needing not to beg the privilege—
Crossed neighbor Allyn's meadow to his row
Of sandknolls; then, as all the cattle go,
Between the roundest couple home to tea.
So Saturday, and night, when we agree
What games shall silence evening, and what talk
Shall bring the ghost whose breast is brittle chalk.
So Sunday, with a visit to the great
Grandfather pine that guards the burial gate.
Neglected there, the town's first graveyard lies
Where once the Hurlburt roadway took the rise,
Bringing a country mourner up to pray.
But year by year the woodchucks have their way,
And higher mounds are there than used to reckon
The small well-buried length of smith or deacon.
So all the week-end over, and the pair
Departed; and a blizzard in the air.

* * * That second snow fulfilled us while it lasted.
But now for two brown weeks the fields have fasted
Under a windless, under a lukewarm sun.
Christmas Eve and New Year's Day are done,
And here we stand expectant, straining dumbly
Toward a long stretch that will not lie so comely—
Three dark, inclement months before the spring.

Or such the hope; we want no softer thing,
No disappointment deepened day by day.
That second snow, dissolving, drained away
Too much of sudden glory, and too much
Of the towered god whose mantle we must touch.
There was no blizzard in it after all.
Only a thickening sky, so slow to fall
That Monday passed, and Tuesday. Then a hush;
Then a faint flick, as if a fox's brush
Had gained the woods in safety, and the hole;
Then steadily, steadily down the winter stole.
All afternoon it hissed among some clump
Of shrubbery, and deepened round the pump;
All afternoon, till time put out the light.
Then the black rustling through the soundless night—
Dark flake on flake colliding where no gaze
Of beast or person followed. Dim the ways
Of snow in great high darkness; strange the sound
Of whiteness come invisible to ground.
And yet the lamps awhile allowed the glance
Of a stray whirl of moth wings blown to dance,
Confused, beyond the four and twenty panes.
Here once we sat and watched the autumn rains
Stitching a wall of water. Now the snow—
A frailer fall, and gentler—came to sew
New raiment for the sun-accustomed sashes.
The upstairs window that a north wind lashes,
Beating the maple on it gust by gust,
Hung silent, like a picture; but it thrust
Pure light on brilliant branches, layered well
With silver that as slowly rose and fell,
No visible lawn beneath it, and no thing,

Round or above, save blackness in a ring:
A prone, suspended skeleton creeping hither,
All knuckle joints and bare bones twigged together.
Next morning then, with Christmas five days off,
What wonder if we called this well enough?
What wonder if the two boys prematurely
Counted upon continuance, and surely
Bragged of a snowy hill for him, the guest—
The expected boy, of all their friends the best,
Due now from deep Virginia on a night—
Their own, to play a week with out of sight?
So off they hurried, pulling the sleds behind them,
To cross the nearest meadow-stretch and find them
Somewhere a perfect slope that they could pack—
The runners for the hundredth time and back
Deep-sinking through the softness, with dragged feet
To finish a rough design and leave it neat.
I watched them for a little from the road,
Then called, and she came with me to the snowed
White forest edge, and over the wall inspected
The prints of birds; or how a deer directed
Leap after leap to gain his inland thicket.
A pine branch sagged to the earth, but I could flick it,
Filling my neck with flakes as up it reared,
Snow-loosened of its many-pointed beard.
Meanwhile the cry of coasters over the hill,
With moment interruptions, clear and still,
That said the feet were staggering up again.
We came, and Sam the wolf-dog joined them then
In a loud, urgent welcome, bark and word.
For he had crossed the field to make a third,
And close-pursued them, snapping at their feet

Now up the slope, now down—then off to meet
Plump Snappy, most companionable cat,
Who, plowing the snow alone, arrived and sat
Like something stone of Egypt, not for play.
He watched us, two by two, slide swift away,
Then turned his head, encouraging the weak one,
Snippy, the little sister, the grey meek one,
Who half from home had squatted in a track;
And wailed until we saved her, walking back.
That was the day, with four days still to come,
We prophesied long whiteness—hearing the hum
Of trees contracted slowly in no wind;
Or watching the clouds a clear sun dipped and thinned.
That was the night the low moon, all but waned,
Came to me once—upstarting at the strained
Hurt sound of something strangled in the woods—
Came to me at the window, over floods
Of waveless shining silence, and I said:
There is a month of coldness dead ahead.
But Thursday of a sudden thawed it all,
And Friday, like a silly thing of fall,
An innocent late-summer thing, declared
Calm days, with every melting meadow bared.
So when they blew their horn and gained the gate—
Those weary three Virginians—only a late
Cool breath of proper evening blew to greet them.
Sam leapt out ahead of us to meet them.
Then the old rejoicing, four and three;
With talk of the north till bedtime, and the tree
We all must bring tomorrow—a picked pine
To anchor in a room with block and twine.
We found it, best of several by a swamp,

And sawed and bore it hither amid the romp
Of boys and tumbling cats, that on warm haunches
Settled to watch us trim the bristling branches;
Looping the ends with silver-studded cord
And lo, with more than patience could afford
Of cranberries and popcorn needled through—
Now red, now white, now one and one, and two!
From every room, when darkness well was down,
Came packages of mystery, in brown
Creased paper if a boy or man were giver;
But if a lady, candle-light would quiver
On multicolored tissue, gold and green.
Then silence, with a glow behind the screen
To point our way to bed, the lamps unlighted.
Then dawn, and stairs acreak, and something sighted
Even beyond the door that we had closed;
Then breakfast, and the mysteries deposed—
No more the ache of waiting; shed the power
Preeminent of any future hour.
That was the height; the rest was going down,
With random walks, or driving into town,
Or sitting after sunfall over tea.
We tidied rooms and set the spangled tree
Midway the snowless lawn, and spiked it there—
Popcorn and berries on it, and a square
Of suet tied with string to tempt the flying
Birds. But there were kittens always spying,
Ready to pounce and punish; and at last
A brief wind laid it over like a mast.
The rest was milder pleasure, suiting well
Our seven tongues that had so much to tell.
We talked. And then the final day was come.

Farewell, you three! And if the end was dumb,
Remember this—there was no charm to say
As down the hill your fenders sloped away.
So Christmas Eve and New Year's Day are done;
And still the lukewarm, still the windless sun
Possesses what it watches—hidden here,
A barn and painted house, from which appear
Four little figures scanning a clear sky.
It doubtless will be clouded by and by,
And doubtless yield each one his small desire.
Now only tracks, minute upon the mire.

* * * O welcome night-wind, crazily arriving,
You had not warned us till we heard you striving,
Here and at every corner of the house—
Now a great beast and now a nibbling mouse—
Striving in every stature to undo us;
There was no rumor of your marching to us,
No swift annunciation; or eight hands
Loud, loud had hailed you, giving you our lands,
Ourselves, and all this valley to unsettle.
We only lay and heard you—heard the rattle
Of shutters, and caught the groan as you went on
Of nails from weather-boarding all but drawn.
We only lay, pulling the covers higher,
Until at dayrise, grouping about the fire,
We greeted a hundred frost-hills on the panes;
Looked through, and saw the still wind-worried lanes
Thrash heavily; and walking out a little,
Said the snapped, hanging branches were wind-spittle.
Nor was the blowing over; still at twelve
High limbs were double-curving, like a helve,

And through the day, beneath white clouds and round ones,
All was a sea, with us the happy drowned ones—
Drifting among the layers of thin cold,
Self-separated. Some, the slow and old,
Slid lazily, floating beyond a world;
But some were childish-violent, and curled
And slapped our willing foreheads as they raced.
Layer upon clear layer built a waste
Of space for minds to work in, high and low.
Then the loud night that bade the softness go—
With iron for morning ground, and every print
Of dog or man foot stamped as in a mint:
All metal, all eternal, if this cold,
High, many-shelving universe could hold.
It held; and laid a film across the pond;
Laid more, and laying others, brought the fond
Brown wolf-dog there to slide beside the boys—
Bewildered, but enchanted by the noise
Of brittle alder-sticks and clapping hands.
So now the ice in hourly thickened bands
Is pressing tight around us, pond and lawn.
One moment, and the mighty gale was gone,
Far-whistling. Then a silence, and the fall
To nothing. Then the crisp iron over all.

* * * Slap, slap, the sound of car chains going by,
With elsewhere only stillness, under dry
Fantastic heaps of white the wind renews.
It reached us evenly, as snowfalls use;
But there were days of fury when the air,
Whirled white as flour, was powdery everywhere;
Till now the finest grains, like desert sand,

Wait upon eddies they will not withstand.
The snow-plows on the highway come and go—
Not vainly, but a devil takes the snow
Some windy times, and then the car lanes fill
Along the leeward side of fence or hill.
The boys are in the snow house we had made
Before this blowing weather overlaid
The first wet fall with something crisp as salt.
Four walls we packed without a single fault
Between a pair of solid shutter forms.
A roof, an eastern door away from storms,
Two windows at the ends—a bread knife cut them,
Neatly, but there was then no way to shut them—
A piece of crate for cushion, and a bag:
This is their windy fortress that a flag
Flies every day in front of, and that Sam
Lies guarding—less the dragon than the lamb.
There was a man with anthracite for eyes,
And pennies for his buttons; but he lies,
Forgotten, uncreated, where he fell.
There was a castle wall beyond the well
With store of snowballs piled against a siege,
And apples for the starving, lord or liege;
But now it too is levelled, and delight
Dwells only in this hovel at the right.
Below the sheds and halfway to the wall
Stands a lean ice house, windowless and tall,
Whose ancient door hung open day by day
Till the last shining cake was stowed away.
When ice was fourteen inches teams were hitched;
Saws buzzed; and like a waterland bewitched
The silver floor divided, line and angle.

Then loaded trucks, with pairs of tongs to dangle,
Teasing the helpful boys until they tried—
Slipped, fell, and were convinced. And so inside
Sleep twice a hundred pieces of the pond,
Preserved against the dog days and beyond.

* * * These are the undistinguishable days.
This is the calm dead center of the maze
Whereinto we have wandered, and in time
Shall wander forth again, and slowly climb
A wall the other side of which is change.
Now everything is like, with nothing strange
To keep our hands aware of what they do.
This is the winter's heart, that must renew
Its steady, steady beating when an embered
Joy is all we have, and thoughts remembered.
Therefore do I listen while I may,
Monotony, to what your whispers say
Of systole, diastole, and the ribbed
Sweet rituals wherein our wills are cribbed.
Therefore shall I count the doings here
Of one full day, and represent the year.

We rise at eight, but I an hour before
Have put the pipeless furnace in a roar—
Descending slow in slippers, robe, and socks
To where, as in some Southern ship that rocks,
Dry cargo-wood inhabits all the hold.
Our destination only the days unfold—
Tier on tier down-sloping to warm weather.
But many a hundred chunks lie yet together,

Snug in their odorous rows. So I inspire
Last evening's spent and barely-breathing fire;
Pull off my gloves; ascend the under-stair;
And smoke a chilly moment in a chair.
Then up again. But they are coming down,
Each head of hair in tangles at the crown;
And suddenly we smell a breakfast waiting—
Bacon and yellow eggs; or, alternating,
Buckwheat cakes with butter for anointing;
Or third-day porridge, grey and disappointing.
Prepared with steaming water and the comb,
We gather about the range—the morning home
Of kittens, too, and Sam the wolf-dog, stretched
Full length behind it while our plates are fetched.
The Irish hands that laid our dining table
Were up in early darkness, whence a fable
Of ghost or saint, night-walking, has its rise.
We listen, masked amusement in our eyes,
And finishing our fare, proceed to measure
Whether this day is planned for work or pleasure.
There is a woodshed faucet where I fill
Two water pails, and through the winter-still
Bound morning beat the music that she loves—
The restless mare whose foretop, smoothed with gloves,
Will hang with hay-stalk in it while she drinks.
She knows my coming footfall, and she thinks
To speed her slave's arrival with a neigh.
I am too proud to hurry; yet the hay
Seems due her, and the water, none the less.
So up to where last summer's grasses press
Their rustling weight on weight; and casting down
High pitchforkfuls, I stuff the slats with brown,

Stiff breakfast which the clever ponies hear.
I listen to their trotting, small and clear,
Round the curved path to where the western door
Stands open night or day, whatever roar
Of winds or pelt of snow drives ruthless in.
They are from northern islands where the din
Of winter never daunts them. Unconfined,
They wander about the paddock till the mined
Mute hayfall wakes their wisdom. Then they race—
Two blown and hairy creatures—into place.
I leave them there, slow-nibbling, eyes astare,
And go to prod the motor in his lair:
Four thousand pounds inert, and chilled so well
Some mornings I can barely solve the spell.
I have been baffled when a weakened spark
Has failed to fire the monster, and the dark
Webbed shadows of the room have missed his roar.
I have discovered drifts against the door,
And shovelled; I have watched a winter's rains
Turn ice, and been in misery with chains—
Now on, now off, now broken and now mended;
I have as often wished a year were ended.
But now the long thing moves, and backing out
Brings Sam, who disobeys my daily shout
And lopes to where the open meadows tempt him.
I could be angry, but his ears exempt him,
Waiting erect and friendly when I come.
My way was longer round; but now the strum
Of pistons will be answered by his feet,
That guide me to the milkhouse, dark, unneat,
Where the day's pail awaits me. Then the mile
Retravelled—past the cemetery stile

That leads among the six-foot frozen mounds.
There have been mornings when I heard the sounds
Of pick and frozen shovel at a grave;
But mostly snow and timeless silence—save
That cries of farmer children ring in the wood,
Where the white Hollow school long years has stood.
Some of them wave and call my distant name;
Then bells, and marching in to serious game;
While I at my own corner mount the hill
Past Bailey's house, and hers, where now a still
White shaft of smoke that bends above the brook
Declares Grandmother up. A pause; a look;
Good morning to her, cheerful at the door;
Then on to where the barn receives the roar
Of cylinders again until they cease.
Now to the restless mare, whom I release—
High stepping, in perpetual surprise—
To where the ponies shake their shaggy eyes.
All day will they be three beyond a gate,
Ground-musical, and free of their estate;
While we that own them, in and out of doors
Must labor at our self-appointed chores.
Now the grey tool house where the chisels hang,
And hammers lie, and saws with sharpened fang
Rest nightly on their nails, invites my skill.
I am no maker, but a floor can fill
With shavings from the least instructed plane.
Or there is wood to split, come snow or rain,
When the black stove grows hungry, and the dry
Deep kitchen box demands a fresh supply.
Ten times the barrow, loaded, piles its pieces
High at the woodshed end, till all the creases

Fold a fair week of darkness, and the dented
Chopping block is with cold wounds contented.
There is one root the garden still can give.
Under the snow, under the stubble live
Our golden parsnips, planted and forgotten.
Nothing of them is altered or frost-rotten.
The blunt pick thuds in the ground, and up they heave:
A miracle for winter to believe.
I bring them in for dinner on this day;
And while the kettle, boiling their ice away,
Fills half a room with steam I take the road
Once more, to curiosity's abode—
That box where now the mail man will have been.
Arriving slow, I thrust my fingers in;
Draw letters forth, a bundle, or a card;
And out of time abstracted pace the hard
White ground again to where three wait for me.
No ancient courier with a king's decree
Rode ever up a hill and brought so much
As these chilled messages the mind can touch,
Restoring warmth, reviving every word
That yesterday with its own motion stirred.
Meanwhile the boys have had their little school—
Two pupils and a mother, mild of rule,
Who after beds were made and dinner planned,
Called them to where the home-built easels stand
And where the primer waits that one can read.
The younger mind admits a younger need:
Long blocks that tilt together till a boat
Sits sailing; or a castle with a moat;
Or dungeon towers to keep a kitten in—
The almond-eyed four-footed Saracen.

To painting then—tongues out and foreheads glowing,
With bannerets of bright vermilion flowing
Over and up and down; or blues, or blacks,
Full to the very corners past the tacks.
One thing remains: a paragraph to trace
On paper from the blackboard's printed face.
The boy leans long upon the table leaf,
Procrastinating; for the task was brief,
And both of them had still an hour to play.
But there he leans, unwilling, till the day
Brings twelve; and half-past twelve; and brings the white
Sealed letters that are now the noon's delight.
So dinner, and a nap for everyone
Where neither snow may enter nor the sun.
So then the afternoon, that still is short—
Midwinter lags behind the sky's report:
Each day a little longer, but the dark
Comes down before a coaster may remark.
While there is light we seek the genial store,
Off by the covered bridge; or wanting more,
Ride over two east ranges to the town
Of brass that bore the body of John Brown.
Here pavements like a puzzle run and spread;
And here a shop front, gold by gaudy red,
Demands immediate entrance; for a dime
Buys anything, land-born or maritime:
A ball, a wooden car, a masted boat,
An outboard motor that will never float;
A magnet's curve, completed by a bar;
A leaden blue policeman with his star.
So home across the ranges, past the edge
Of evening, till the last high-drifted hedge

Declares the clear necessity of chains.
So out to frosty spokes and windy lanes
Where the snow, blowing, whips the wrist and scatters;
Then upward, while a broken chain-link clatters;
Upward into the barn, the engine dying
Soundless; but the ponies are replying,
Huddled before the big one at the gate.
Scarcely we listen, for we estimate
Two hours this side of supper. Time for tea!
We light the lamps and sip the mystery,
Cup after shadowy cup, with toasted cheese.
There are no country moments like to these;
When afternoon is night, and night belongs
Like a dark heirloom of descended songs
To four that sit in solitude and hear them
Through the fond nothingness that nestles near them.
From the warm circle of the shaded lamp
At last I walk to where the ponies stamp
And the tall guardian mare is loud with thirst.
A boy with lighted lantern sheds the first
Long pair of scantling shadows on the snow;
While I, the water-bearer, dimly go
Through the great backward crescent drawn behind us.
There have been evenings when she would not mind us—
The lurking mare, complacent down the meadow.
But now a clear low whistle cleaves her shadow,
Precipitately arriving. So we lead her,
Plunging, past the corner post; and heed her
Sighing as she nuzzles in the pail.
The lantern from a high and rusty nail
Swings gently, casting circles on the hay.
The kittens somewhere, noiselessly at play,

Keep watch of us, and scan the waiting door.
They love a barn, but love the kitchen more;
And lessons still may linger in each mind
Of the long milkless night they sat confined.
We leave the ponies munching in their room
And blow our lantern black, resolved to come
By starlight home—Orion and the Bears
Low-shining; but aloft upon the stairs,
Bright Castor holding Pollux by the hand.
Now endless evening, like a painted band,
Starts moving, moving past us, and we seize,
Soft-reaching, all that momently can please.
There is an hour for singing, when the book
Lies open, and a rolling eye may look
For prompting at the words of Nelly Gray,
Darby and Joan, The Miller, Old Dog Tray;
Malbrouck that went to war, and Hoosen Johnny;
Or over the ocean, over the sea my bonnie.
The dominoes that once amused us well
Lie in their box and envy bagatelle,
Whose twenty balls, thrust up the tilted board,
Pause and return—click, click—a thousand scored!
With game or song the clock goes round to eight:
Past time for two to sleep, whose laggard gait
We must not hope to hurry up the landing.
Each elder then knows where a book is standing,
Tall on the crowded table; and begins
What may go on until the darkness thins—
Page after page upturned against the light.
For so it was, on such a nipping night,
That Holmes, or Doctor Thorndyke, heard the bell
And raced with lawless death to Camberwell;

Or Watson, in an alley with his master,
Felt the steel fingers as a crutch came faster—
Tapping, tapping, tapping, till the court
Blazed with a sudden pistol's blind report.
This is the hour, and this the placeless room
For smooth concocted tales of lust and doom;
This the remote, the sanctuary year
When the safe soul must fabricate a fear.
Many a milder evening passes, too,
With Royal Casino, Rummy, and a few
Swift-changing hands of High-Low-Jack-and-the-Game.
But then three weeks ago the chess men came;
Since when, no night so busy that it misses
The march of angry Queens, whose scalloped tresses,
Stiffly erected, fly to guard a King.
We are two novices, and rashly fling
Pawns, bishops, knights, and rooks into the fray;
Yet time and blood have taught us wiser play.
There was a gift at Christmas time of Tarot—
Untaught, but we can shuffle them and harrow
A loreless mind with him, the Hanging Man;
So all those numbered mysteries that plan
What future folds the player, and what past
Is carved upon the great Tower overcast,
So every wand and pentacle and sword
Lies curious, unfathomed, on the board.
We have been known, as never back in town,
To idle till the clock weights settled down,
And till the sound of ticking ceased unheard.
We have rejoiced some evenings at the word
Of neighbors driving over; when the names,
Smith, Prentice, Landeck, interrupted games

With something else of equal clear delight.
For there was talking now into the night,
With news of health, and trips away from home,
And how the kitchen beer went all to foam.
Gossip of Hautboy, Dibble, and Great Hill,
Gossip and jest and argument—until:
Goodbye, Smith, Landeck, Prentice; come again;
Goodnight. And so a day is ended then.
Each four and twenty hours, until we rise,
Go thus. And thus the holy winter flies.

* * * February flies, with little summers
Hidden in its beard: unlicensed mummers
Performing April antics for a day.
The sun from the horizon swings away;
The sky melts upward, and a windless hand
Scatters the seeds of warmth along the land.
They will not grow, for ice is underneath,
And every creature tastes it. But a wreath
Lies thrown by playful chance upon the smiling
Meadows that a season is beguiling.
Today was so, but we were not deceived;
Though what the wolf-dog and the cats believed
There is no art of knowing. They pursued
Our every venturing step and found it good:
Down the crisp meadows to the aspen grove;
Over the highway, where a salesman drove
Dry wheels on dry macadam; then the neck
Of Harrison's pasture to the Hollenbeck.
We stood, the seven walkers, on a stone
And watched the river, waveless and alone,

Go slipping, slipping under, gravelly clear.
Snippy, a mile from nowhere, crouched to peer
At nothing in the sand; then bolder sat.
Three weeks, we said, and she would be a cat
With fearsome crying kittens of her own.
Ten months with us—no more—and nearly grown!
So Snappy, arriving plump and solemn there,
Good-natured sat, the guardian of the pair.
There was a barn foundation to explore,
Ancient of fields beyond. The rotting floor
Forewarned us, and we did not enter in;
But strolled, and where tall timothy had been
Lay half an hour on stubble under the sun;
While Sam, excited by a scent, must run
Low-whining up the fences; till a voice
Recalled him, and we made the hapless choice
Of eastward marshy meadows for return.
The hummocks mired us, but a cat could learn
The causeway's secret truth; and what we lost
Came back to us at home with tea and toast.

* * * Since yesterday a hundred years have gone.
The fore-and-after season, living on,
Rouses itself and finds its bitter breath.
This wind holds on to winter as to death.
There is no end, we say, and sauntering out,
Northwestward lean till we are whirled about,
Mute neck and shoulders stinging with the snow;
Or on this Sunday morning think to go,
Foot-heavy, where the giant maples spread
Their smooth enormous branches, long since dead.
Still in this waste of wind they do not fall;

But stiffen, like old serpents sent to crawl
On dense, on layered air; until the charm
Is lifted, and descending out of harm,
They lie leaf-covered, rigid in decay
Until the last small worm has turned away.
Here in the woodland clearings they patrol,
The wind drives steadily upon its goal.
But yonder where the hemlocks lace together
There is a sudden calm, a death of weather.
The shade is black, as once in late July
When here we walked escaping yellow sky.
The shade is black and even, and the snow
Comes filtered to the open cones below—
Slowly, slowly, slowly; strange the hush,
Here in this darkened desert of the thrush.
No hermits now; yet bands of chickadees
Tread fearless of us, chirping in the trees.
The ferns of June are withered on the rocks
Midway the icy stream that bends and locks
This needled promontory where we stand.
Oh happy time! when nothing makes demand;
When all the earth, surrendering its strength,
Regains a taller potency at length;
Sleeps on in purest might of nothing done
Till summer heaves on high the exacting sun.

* * * Ice everywhere, a comic inch of it.
Four veteran walkers of a sudden sit
Wide-sprawling; but the cat that went so sure
Waits in the shed, distrustful and demure.
On this one day the dark mare, left inside,
Stands munching while the startled ponies slide—

Their path a river, and the river frozen—
Until a barn's captivity is chosen.
Ice everywhere; but over Goshen way
Ice on the mountains—murderous display.
Down the wild road to where the lanes were dry
We crept on crunching chains; then letting fly,
Passed houses till we gained the known plateau.
Yet now no more familiar, for the glow
Of crystals, like an ocean, blinded eyes
Untutored in the way a forest dies—
Slim birch and maple, sycamore and larch
Bent low before the mysteries of March;
Bent glassy-low, or splintered to a heap
Of glittering fragments that the sunrays sweep—
The sun, ironic, heartless, come to glance
At death and beauty shivering in a dance.

* * * I have been absent through the ending days
Of March beyond the mountains, where the ways
Of all the world drive onward as before.
I have been absent from the windy door;
Have gazed on travel-mornings out of flying
Windows at a distant winter dying.
But not our own, I said; and still believe
There will be news at home of its reprieve.
Nothing of that can change. And yet the doubt
Creeps into me as I look homesick out
On farms that are reminding me of one—
Not distant now, beneath the selfsame sun.
A further valley, and a further range,
And I shall see if anything be strange.
Another dozen stations, and the three

I have been absent from will run to me—
And tell me if they know. At which the tears
Come premature, and stillness stops my ears.

* * * That very Wednesday, going to Great Hill,
The ruts all melted and the road was swill;
The hub caps foundered, and a number plate
Rose out of mire to recognize the spate.
All underground was overflowing for us,
Helpless until a wakened workhorse bore us,
Backward, absurd, to dry macadam land.
So April, with a wild unwelcome hand,
Showers proof upon us here of winter gone.
Our visitors on Friday night are wan—
Town-tired, and do not know it till we tell them.
The stripling cats, until we thought to bell them,
Havocked among the juncos, dropped to feed
On what the lawn still held of husk or seed.
A hundred misty bellies and blue backs
Move unmolested northward, leaving tracks
On certain darker mornings when a flurry
Satins the ground—not deep enough to worry
Those busy bills that, helped by hopping feet,
Find out the fruit of barberries and eat.
The apple barrels, picked over, have revealed
How many Baldwins never will be peeled;
The fungus spreads, and spots of deathly white
Show where the teeth of time have been to bite.
The wolf-dog has abandoned us by day;
He is in love across the scented way.
Nothing can keep him when the wind arrives;
He chews his chain, or alternately strives

Till the round collar slips and he goes running.
The ponies' noses have as old a cunning.
There is no forage yet, but they can smell
Green tropics creeping hither, and will fell
Each night a length of fence for dumb escape;
Then stumble back at breakfast time and gape,
Wit-withered, at the breach they cannot solve.
So, as the weeks implacably revolve
Of early, windy April, come the sprays
Of wood viburnum in the pathless ways
Where rocks and bent witch-hazel boughs declare
Once more their truce, awakening to air.
So, as the world turned sunward, Snippy died.
In the dim middle of a night she cried,
Desperate upon the steps; and lived a day.
But we have laid her slenderly away.
Her young within her she was not to bear;
So Snappy sits disconsolately there,
Under the branching crabtree; faced about,
Fixed on the clods, as if to stare her out.

* * * Spring is not yet; though how can this be long:
This crush of silence, this untimely-wrong,
Wide, cruel weight of whiteness, wing-descended
Even as we declared the winter ended?
Last night it happened. Everything, unwarned,
Suffered the soundless swoop of him the Horned,
The Universal Owl, whose ruthless plumes
Settled like death, distributing our dooms;
No feather heavy, but the sum of all
Seemed ultimate—earth's sepulchre and pall.
Not a flake settled on the flimsiest twig

But stayed; until this morning all were big
With monstrous moveless worms, that in the sun
Drip swiftly; but the evil has been done.
How fair it was last evening, when our lamp
Shone out on fleecy lilacs; yet the damp,
The clammy hand of this last dying snow—
How terrible to touch, and inly know:
This is the breaking end. So now at noon,
Divided, we behold the orchard strewn
With murdered buds and down-demolished branches.
So, by the graveyard, death upon its haunches
Sits in the form of great-grandfather-pine's
Chiefest of giant limbs, whose blackened lines
Trace there a new design of death across
Bare stones for whom no novelty of loss,
No morning news of woe can tell them more
Than that another winter shuts the door.
Divided thus—admiring, yet appalled—
We watch the season, poor, unfuneralled,
Pass with no mourners on; and recognize
What most we loved here impotent to rise.
If any sight could soften us to spring,
It is this melted, this emaciate thing.

* * * So April's plumefall was the last one, leaving
Nothing behind save midmonth warmth, and heaving
Roots, rain-drenched on many a sodden day.
Now even the rain is gone, that kept us grey—
Even the rain, preserving darkness too.
After the flood dry weather, hot and blue,
Washed every stain of winter off, and brightly
Gave us this world, so changeable and sightly:

Grass upon the mountains; smokeless-green
May fire that will not languish till the lean,
Brown, bitten earth, monotonous with stone,
Hides under hotness, leafy and alone;
Shade everywhere—as here beneath the crab,
Where Snippy lies, and rumors of Queen Mab
Bring bees to set the blossoms in a roar
While marvelling children pace the petalled floor;
Shade then for her, the borrowed Tabby, lying
With three new kittens, curious and crying—
The summer's offspring, not to be confused
With those somehow more brave that March misused.
Now the sleek mare is shod again, and trots
Each day beneath her mistress, over lots
Green-rising, or along a sandy road:
Each of them glad, the bearer and the load;
But I that walk to meet them down the lawn
Remember lazy mornings lost and gone—
Remember the cold, remember the lantern, hanging
There by her nose at night, and blizzards banging
Somewhere a shabby door; and my decision
Goes to the old, the February vision.
How old it is now, only a rake and spade;
Only a wolf-dog, panting in the shade;
Only a coatless, an oblivious pair
Of boys for whom all days to come are fair;
Only her warm hand, patting down the seed
Where sunlight lingers and the frost is freed;
Only the hay-land, live again with snakes;
Only these things can say what memory aches—
Oh, vainly—to recapture; only such
Can tell of the holy time our blood will touch—

Oh, never again, and never; only June,
That sings of something over deathly soon.
Already the mind's forgetfulness has blended
Music with music; and the months are ended.

SONNETS

I

I said: It will not blow this way again;
The branches of my life too soon are old;
The wind is kind to early-withered men
Lest they remember and confess the cold.
I said, and scarcely knew that it was I,
Hanging my leaves there in the springless year.
I said; and did not listen to a high,
Loud sound of March that filled the woods with fear.
Then it was all around me, till at last
Love like a hurricane of hate was blowing—
Bruising me everywhere. Yet I was fast,
And stood among the ruins of his going.
  Only the after stillness came and showed
  These blossoms on me everywhere, like blood.

II

No wonder-deed done in the oldest time
Whose whiteness burns oblivion away,
No miracle of grass, whose muted rhyme
Outsings the dawn and silences the jay,
No fiend's invention, no good man's endeavor,
No other tale of love is so untrue
As this one of my heart, that empties never,
But fills even as you take, and still is new.
It cannot be there is more love to come;
Yet, coming on, love tells me I have lied.
So I must learn to listen and grow dumb,
Believing in a heart that never died—
  Believing then in you, who like a dream
  Draw out of me this ever waking stream.

III

You may grow tired of my incessant tongue,
That loves perhaps too well the work of praise.
You may turn otherwhere, and search among
All men for one who keeps the wordless ways.
This you may do, and I admit the fault
Of loving you too wakefully to cease.
Oh, I have tried to mend me, but the salt
Of silence never brought these lips release.
Still must they harken to the thoughts behind
That form and flow to utter your perfection.
Still must they move before a driven mind
Marching to death in your unchanged direction.
  Therefore at least I bind them with one thong,
  This reticence that wraps a formal song.

IV

As if there lay one other sky beyond
This sky that was enough for any man;
As if the midnight bloomed, and frond on frond
Of blackness waved across Aldebaran;
Or the bent miser, opening his box,
Found double gold; or some most comely youth,
Walking at noon, caught light among his locks,
And the sun paled, impoverished of truth;
So is the love that fills me an excess,
Unlacked before, unwaited till it came;
Unneeded now—but oh the mind's distress
If it should lose one letter of your name!
   If nature strolled with her proportioning knife
   And pruned this farthest limb that is my life!

V

No throat had ever told me what I know,
And knowing now so well, pity a lover's
Silence; for the voice of love is low;
It cannot rise to what the heart discovers.
It cannot sing as high as love's own mind,
Which, truant among birds, flies daily back
With a wide restlessness, and looks behind
At everything the darkened house will lack.
Therefore I hold these words inside my heart,
Therefore I tie each thought that would ascend.
They languish, but it is the better part,
And there is sweeter music in the end—
    Unheard by even you, on whom the sound
    Gathers like dew upon the senseless ground.

VI

Chasten your fears, I have not been destroyed,
All that was in me once is living still;
Only I know there was this slender void,
This threading vein through an unconscious hill.
Empty of you, it nourished every part
With nothingness, and I was none the worse.
Filled with you suddenly, it is the start
Of older riches than I can rehearse—
Joy like a hidden river that no stone
Ever is worn away by where it runs;
Peace in the darkest passages of bone,
And buried light as from a hundred suns;
  With tolerance, that sweetens as it flows
  This blood whose red remembers late the rose.

VII

That you were there to see before I saw,
Midway the range of old day-lighted things,
That you were there, and so by vision's law
The truth of you went off in widened rings;
That you lived ever in such early time
Is past my understanding, save that now,
This evening, I have seen the day-stars climb
Down step by step of darkness; and I vow,
No more than you they needed night between,
No more than you they watched the world away—
As here upon no earth I stand and lean,
Loving your light that is the end of day;
With no beginning after, for the dawn
Was grey, and I am glad that it is gone.

VIII

When I am called by Love to give account
Of the one thing that holds me unto you,
I will obey him to the strict amount;
One nameless thing I know, and it must do.
I will tell Love how first you looked at me—
Head down, and something level in your eyes;
How still you stood and looked; and I could see
Half-risen modesty, to rule surprise;
How then you spoke, and how your voice was low,
And how your arms hung perfectly await.
I will ask Love himself to pause and go,
And look, and understand my changeless state—
  Rooted again within your level gaze,
  Eternal now across the evening ways.

IX

All of the steps that our slow love has taken
Were your own steps at last, who led the way.
I was too fixed—or like an oak was shaken
That has been marked to fall yet never may.
Never unless you taught me had I known it:
Love must be advancing or it dies.
You found each resting-place, but had outgrown it
Before I too was ready to arise.
Love is a journey to no end, except
One traveller, halting, cannot journey more.
When I awoke you had as wisely stepped
As the sole fox across a forest floor;
So I would always follow you; and will
To the last hedge upon the highest hill.

X

The time not spent in kissing you is chaff
Gone windily away; is desert bones;
Is the lost acorn; the discarded half
Of ore from which were plucked the golden stones;
Is air beyond our breathing; is the dust
That rings another world, nor brings it rain;
Is worse than nothing had—the final crust
Was there, and it was fatal to refrain.
So have I said, yet it was never true.
Poor talk, you had your uses all the while.
Slow words, between your pauses hung the two
Far eyes I had forgotten, and the smile.
  Not that I had forgotten; but the heart
  Grows blind if it too seldom holds apart.

XI

Where is the wit that I could sometimes wield—
And yours, for you were happier than I?
Where is the hand that held the tapered shield,
Daring the sharpest arrows to let fly?
My wrists are down, I am without defense,
And what is worse, incompetent to wound;
My regiments are sleeping in their tents;
My talk at last is gentle and untuned.
And yours, for you were readier to strike,
And sat upon the swifter-coming horse—
Now do you understand what love is like?
I think he cannot even feel remorse,
  This mischievous small killer in the dark
  Who cuts two living tongues out for a lark.

XII

I disagreed, and you misunderstood,
And the sick moments dragged their wings along.
What matters, though, one worm within the wood,
What matters one rude note within the song?
There still is all of time, wherein this hour
Will sweeten as it ages and be relished.
Love is no love that lacks the bitter power
With its own ugliness to be embellished.
There still is all of song, that will enclose
These wounded wings and heal them till they lift,
And the worm sleep, and the musician doze—
Swooning to hear a melody so swift
   That no one there can guess the happy hand,
   Save you and me, who both will understand.

XIII

Come with me Love and listen all the while,
And warn me if I say too much again.
She cannot see that I am bare of guile,
Or that there grow as many loves as men.
She cannot estimate my love is me.
She takes me as I am, but it should alter.
It should be tentative, observe degree,
And in a kind of greenness never falter.
So come with me and watch my ripened tongue,
For I am willing now that she be suited;
Let her believe that I am only hung
With blossoms that so heavily am fruited.
  Then in good time she may accept my words;
  Unless the worms have had them, and the birds.

XIV

I was confused; I cannot promise more
This morning than to keep these miles between us.
I can do that, although the heart grow sore
And the night weep for ever having seen us.
I can do that; but I will not engage
To come and slay this love before your eyes.
Let it die here, without the extra wage
Of torture that would shame us everywise.
Let me come afterward—however long—
And say to you I love you none the less.
Nor will I speak of any righted wrong.
Let it be dead, and let us both confess
  With laughter how we fasted forty days
  In the kind wilderness of time's delays.

XV

My love is not endangered by your doubt.
I said it was, but I must now unsay it.
Nothing could be so weak to put it out
As your late words, that only softly sway it—
Returning to this window where it burns,
Night after absent night, to blow it black;
But my more stubborn flame looks up and learns
From stars that even time will not attack.
Such love will bend a little in the wind,
And wisely, if a calm be long away;
But never will you prove that I have sinned
By listening to anything you say;
  Unless you come more ready to receive
  Than give; and let me hear that you believe.

XVI

Should this end now it were the end of light,
That would no longer reach an earth receded;
And the grey death of odor; and a blight
On taste and touch, with every sound unheeded.
I could no longer count the falling days,
Nor weigh an ounce of sorrow out to pain;
It were the end of knowledge when the ways
Of feeling are as reason to the brain.
Should it end suddenly—but I am wrong.
Nothing so invisible can shatter.
Our love is not an object, like the long
Cold hand of time, that is the purest matter.
  But that is something different, and slow,
  And closes gradually, as the senses go.

XVII

Leave me not overlong at this remove;
In the half-darkness, Love, I see too well
My shortness when some measurement shall prove
How far below her hope I always fell.
Keep me no longer, Love, for there is that;
And this, which is more dreadful to attest:
Out of the dusk I have been staring at
Her face is gone that was my only rest.
My dwelling-place, her eyes, cannot be found;
I look, but see as little, coming home,
As the long voyager whose only sound
Is sighing when he finds the ocean foam
  Still hung to make a curtain high and dim
  Between the house of his true life and him.

XVIII

When I came back to your unlifted eyes,
And spoke to you, inquiring how we did,
And you looked up without the least surmise—
Then the old music, that so long was hid,
Sounded; and I knew it was to pour
Forever while we lived, with no abating.
The unskilled players were unskilled no more,
And every string had sweetened by its waiting.
There will be nothing now but one clear tone,
Of which we shall not tire; and when it pauses
We shall exist upon love's faith alone,
That knows all silence to its deepest causes;
  And comprehends the ever devious ways
  I still must follow as I sing your praise.

XIX

I would dislike you if you used an art
To make me love you more than this, the most;
For it is only downward that the heart
Could move from such an eminence—poor boast!
Each day I am confounded, for you give
Each day the wheel of love a little turn;
And I go headlong with it, lest I live
Henceforth one arc behind; and never learn
There is no going downward in our love;
I could not fall and lose you if I tried.
There is no under here, and no above,
But round and round; and distances have died.
  Nor am I ever giddy, for love's air,
  Like this of earth, turns with it everywhere.

XX

How can I prove that I have undersung,
Like you, the written air of our affection?
You do not sing at all, but keep among
Dark words that tell of love by indirection.
And have I sung too high? It is not so.
I rose, but it was never to be reached—
This simplest note that any reed could blow;
Yet not my voice, however it beseeched
Bird, sky, and grass to lend their happy skill,
And every buried lover all his art.
They laughed; and he advised my stubborn will
To cease within the silence of your heart;
  Which I would have it do were I as wise
  As one who had not listened to your eyes.

XXI

Let it be always secret what we say;
And where we meet, be that our world alone.
Nor think us ever guilty, since our day
Is one on which no shadow-bands have shown.
Shame is a shadow that will never fall
On us who have cut down the trees of pride.
Let the world darken past the garden wall;
The space within is conscienceless and wide.
Nor think us ever weary, or in need
Of company to bring the night at last.
Love is a lonely and contented deed,
Done in a desert that is sweet and vast;
  Where neither of us turns a timeless head
  To see the world behind us that is dead.

XXII

As the blue fringes of this flower desire
Comparison; yet even this old glass,
Wherein some workman hid the sky afire,
Is not the same; and so the mind must pass,
And look along the world, and never come
To the pure hue repeated—thus I range
Through the live chronicles that tell the sum
Of love's known history; and each is strange.
No love is like our love beyond the start;
Two look upon each other, then we lose them.
They whisper to each other, but apart,
In a wild shade, and we can never use them—
  Likening ourselves to nothing more
  Than two late comers as the long day wore.

XXIII

Sometimes I fear that I too soon was mastered.
Sometimes I think that you would have me still
Untaken—not like any crippled dastard,
Here with my hands up and my useless will.
Yet I must run the risk of being sure.
I tell you I am captive, every inch;
And was so long ago that I am pure
Even of the memory that pride could flinch,
And look away, and dream of being free.
I tell you this, and ask you then to know,
Nothing so well could prove my high degree,
Nothing so well declare the worthy foe.
I am no more ashamed to kiss the rod
Than the king was, acknowledging the god.

XXIV

What golden spider warmed himself and spun
This web that is the flesh upon your bones—
Warming himself beneath a spicy sun
That caught the winds and let their little moans,
Like woven music, enter every place
To hide until love's fingers should be near?
What artisan was singing at your face?
Who wrapped the rest, that too will disappear?
For time, that made the spinner, lets him die.
He will be long in leaving, yet he must;
So every moistened thread of you will dry—
At first to lace; but then a little dust.
  And I—Oh, time will take my desolate hand
  And sift it on you, letting it be sand.

XXV

I carry in me always, since you live,
The devil of an uncontrolled delight.
He is my hidden master, whom you give
No heed, for he has seldom come in sight.
No passerby may know I am possessed,
And even you will never learn his power.
The host himself is helpless when the guest
Sits on and on, and, smiling hour by hour,
Spreads darkest joy that round him ever flows
Like a sweet, bitter poison. So I keep
This fellow of the smile, and no one knows;
And so it only seems to be asleep—
    My laughter, that the world forever misses;
    Yet here it is, like sun upon our kisses.

XXVI

Oh, I could talk forever, and as smoothly
As angels, were I farther from the fire.
I am the coal, and so I say uncouthly
Less than I mean, and more than you require.
Or if the distance widens on some days,
And I am for the moment swift of tongue,
A sudden sword will stop me on the phrase,
And every sentence after be unstrung.
Or if I once again am well contained,
And cool, as though I grew in watered ground,
The green with which my branches have been veined
Runs red, and I am rooted in the sound
  Of blooming under earth, and blowing cold.
  There is no single way it can be told!

XXVII

My fancy is less cruel than it is kind,
Though cruel it is to bring your spirit here,
Letting it seem your body; for I bind
No arms within these arms when you appear.
They know, and my eyes know, you have been standing
Most of a summer's day beyond the door.
But they have not the magic for commanding
One solid proof: a shadow on the floor.
Your lack of so impalpable a thing
Convinces me at last you never came,
And stood, and looked upon your underling;
Or if you did, my reason was to blame—
    Refusing then to recognize in you
    What such an afternoon might filter through.

XXVIII

The earth is full of spirits once again.
Maidens in the marshes, bearing light,
Laugh the old ones up, the little men;
The ground remembers goblins day and night.
For every standing tree there is a face
That, somewhere hidden, soon must flicker home;
Each mountain side is rippled with the race
Of night-returning devil-face and gnome.
The thought of you is everywhere. It rises
Sometimes like a fiend and stares at me.
I am the helpless savage who devises
Charms; and knows he never will be free.
  Never shall I walk another wood
  Than this of your fixed eyes and pointed hood.

XXIX

Never to be renewed or to increase,
And never to be changed from what it was:
The love that was the maker of this lease
Was love-upon-first-sight, whom all the laws
Of happiness obey, and kingdoms coming
Choose to be the glory of their thrones.
He is the oldest love, he is the humming
Of these incessant bees among my bones;
He is the senses' king; my youngest thought
He molds before I know it has been born;
He is the flesh's despot; the inwrought,
Deep joy; or in my side the sudden thorn.
  Oh, strange that on that day I was so strong,
  Bearing him all at once; and now so long!

XXX

This book declares my love is a condition,
Determined in the tissue; but it lies.
I banish the impertinent physician;
I must refuse to credit one so wise.
Or if there must be fables, let them tell
Of wounds that were inflicted from the flank;
How once we faced each other, and there fell
Swift arrows out of nothing, and they drank
My blood, and put a poison in its place;
My courage, and refilled me with desire;
How then the tincture spread, till into grace
I stumbled, and the punishment of fire—
  Unending, for no heart in all that heaven
  Recovers from a wound the god has given.

XXXI

The longest hour is swifter than I thought.
It is more cruel, having a sharper end.
So time is my close foe; yet I am taught
Some safety by this fear that is my friend—
This fear of eyes that if they ever used
Their utmost power would then I think destroy me;
This awe of something not to be abused,
Lest the world break, and love no more employ me.
For such a fear it is withholds my hands
At the last greedy instant; there I wait,
Lowly, as the shaded hunter stands
And lets the shining pheasant pass in state—
  Something that is too beautiful to miss;
  Yet the dream holds me while the sickles hiss.

XXXII

These things I say, no one of them can reach
The roundness of the sphere that is your truth.
They are but lonely segments, they beseech
Environment and complement. Time's tooth
Devours even while I write; though did it starve,
I still would stand too far from either pole.
Had I eternity, I could but carve
Inscriptions that were partial to the whole.
Not even all together would declare
This roundness, that more swift than words can follow,
Grows, until the mind is thin as air,
And what is most compendious most hollow.
  Better that I should cease, and so re-enter
  Love's little room, revolving at the center.

XXXIII

Not pride it was that made me say so much
Bearing on my own mind in these, your songs.
Intended for your praise, they did but touch
Idea, where your beauty best belongs,
And straightway thought was active, bringing proof,
Here in my heart's possession, of your power.
These but effects; the cause remains aloof;
There is no certain entrance to the tower.
If any gate were open I would climb,
Life-long, and reach your verity at last;
And sing—Oh, I can hear the happy rhyme
Break upward, I can see the overcast
    Part swiftly, and can lose the final sound.
    Alas! I never heard it from this ground.

XXXIV

My only need—you ask me, and I tell you—
Is that henceforth forever you exist.
You are not mine; I may not ever bell you
Like an owned animal for night and mist.
My only need, whatever darkness take me,
Whatever tears close now my separate eyes,
Is that you live, and let the knowledge make me
Immortal as the day that never dies—
That, swift and even, turns into the sun,
As turns the after-shadow down to death.
Let neither then my night, my day be done;
Let them both swing in silence, with no breath
  To call you from the distances you keep.
  (Would they were little; would that my love could sleep!)

THE EYES

The Eyes

Turn where he would that autumn, when the time
Was evening, and there was no wind at all;
Turn where he would he saw them, and he said:
"I am grown old, it is my ending fall;
These are my visitation." Then he smiled.
"They have not seen that I am reconciled.

"They cannot tell me what I first had known.
I learned it long ago, and made surrender.
My bones are at the mercy of the years,
That, coming on, will find as my defender
Nothing but this smile. It cannot harm them,
Though it may shine and for a day disarm them."

As lightly then as this he bore the eyes
That out of every evening stared at him.
Turn where he would they found him; past the door,
Past trees and down the lawn, or through the dim
Road light that bound him in, a noiseless river.
So lightly could he look, so little shiver.

So little did he fear those changeless eyes
That he could fail to see the person changed.
It never was the same tall body there,
Nor the same hair, so carefully arranged—
So perfect and so parted, with a white
Down-line that was indelible by night.

It seemed a woman's hair, and then a man's;
But always it was drawn upon with fire:

Cold fire; and cold the eyes, whatever bones
Held the spare flesh as on a frame of wire—
Dangled, inconstant; but the staring three,
The eyes and that one line, would always be.

Would always be, he said. It was October,
And the last leaf had settled to the lawn.
So the last night was there that he would turn,
Expecting them in silence to have gone.
Would always be. He said it, half aloud,
And trembled; for the rigid one had bowed.

Only an instant, but it seemed enough—
The eyes gone swiftly out, the line erect.
Then the head vanished, and the shoulders flowed
Like a mist backward, till the dusk was specked
With lingerings of terror. So they faded;
And there he stood, implacably invaded.

Turn where he would the face must follow now;
Sleep as he might, his lids come cool together,
Something more cold than peace would enter, slowly,
Like a mist inward, till the mind's calm weather
Ceased, and a shouldered figure gathered form
Out of pressed distance and the soundless storm.

Nor would the eyes that watched him, and the hair—
Unblown, for all was windless there and wild,
Unblinking, for there was no rain to fall
Though the fog drifted and the sky was piled—
Nor would the triple watcher then unfold
Merely the tale of time and growing old.

Something more terrible, for him alone,
Something without a name until he said it.
Yet so far he was tongueless—asking now
What old forgotten guilt had lain and bred it.
Ruthless on the couch of what lost deed.
What wound, that so long afterward could bleed.

What evil? But he ever had been blameless;
He had been praised too sweetly not to know.
There was no saint more mannerly of conscience;
He had stopped short and let the others go—
Stumbling into errors he could see
Too clearly not to shun them. He was free,

And knew it—could remember, could remember
Multitudes of gentlenesses done:
Angers turned away until they withered,
Challenges unpampered, and the one
Deep lust that is the darkener of eyes—
Oh, love had been the better thing, and wise!

With this for past he could outstare the present.
Whatever face it was, he would come smiling,
Tomorrow, after sunset, and implore it
Fiercely to speak. He would himself—beguiling,
With memory at his back—demand the charge;
Then, listening, explain; and be at large.

He was not waited for. The room he lay in—
Stiffened there, with lids too dry to close—
Tilted at some moment after midnight,
Standing him halfway up; so he arose;

Took step; and like a walker in his sleep
Found the whole firmament with eyes acreep.

They moved as if at random, round and round,
And slowly, till he tried to look away;
When, suddenly assembling, they transfixed him
With a cold, single stare, that he must stay
Forever now beneath; as if his life
Lay victim to some never falling knife.

"It will not fall," he said, "it will not fall.
This face will never utter what it knows.
The words I have awaited will deny me
Even a malediction at the close.
The final and the sacrificial jest
Is silence and those eyes along the west.

"Two eyes, and only two, with parted hair
On high to make their mockery more sleek;
More sure my cold confusion, lest I breed
Some courage from that gaze, and stand and speak.
If now I should address that shining sneer—
It will not hear," he said; "it will not hear.

"This mind will never open to my words.
I was convicted easily and well.
Too late for pleading now." And yet he started;
And the black sky became a listening shell,
Contracted in an instant to the size
Of a thin voice beseeching. "Awful eyes—

"More awful that you never yet have closed,
More terrible than any sightless end—

Let down your weight of malice, slowly, swiftly;
Make it in thunder, make it in ice descend,
Make it in mist befoul me, cry me lost;
Spend, spend yourself, although I be the cost!

"I will go under gladly, so I know
One moment of my enemy's close breath.
I can be parted happily from night—
This night—if I but catch the look of death.
Be hideous and torture me, be slow;
Only begin, and let the levers go.

"What engine are you, stealthily devised?
What hand is there, what purpose past the dark?
I beg an instant's vision of the power
So hidden that a world may not remark
How strangely I am visited, how long
I linger in suspension for no wrong.

"No wrong unless you name it, for I say
That I have loathed the bright way and the cruel.
I have seen bodies burning, but the match
Never was mine, and never was I the fuel.
Never have I been thievish after pleasure.
I have kept home, I have respected measure.

"I have not been that plunderer of joy
Who drinks our brother's blood and creeps away;
Letting it dry within him till the rust,
Like a fine crafty poison, spreads decay—
At first a potent hatred, but grey time
Enfeebles it and whitens it to lime.

"I have been bravely diffident, like love;
I have been lawful, keeping our sister's peace.
No lamb has ever huddled to its mother,
Fearing my steps; inviolate the fleece.
Lust ages, but love steadily is younger;
I have been patient, I have not hurried hunger.

"I have not sped the day, oh terrible eyes. . . .
Nor shall I now boast longer. I have ended.
Nor was it boasting, Gazer; it was truth,
With pride and with a little anger blended.
If you have heard me, even the anger goes.
I was exhausted, waiting." He arose,

Still like a walking sleeper, and still waiting;
But no word came for answer from the eyes.
Only they glittered lazily, and gathered
Fragments of mist, gathered them magnet wise,
And wreathed them into smiles, and slowly slept;
While in his weak astonishment he wept.

They would not even trouble to undo him.
Time was long, with evenings still to come.
He looked again; they dozed and were complacent.
He tried to call again, but he was dumb.
It was no world for words, his feet were saying,
Leading him in at last; nor one for praying.

"I will outmock them then," he lay and whispered.
"Tomorrow must I seem indifferent too.
Tomorrow when they waken they must find me
Difficult, unreachable, and new.

I shall not even wonder if they still
Keep station there, wishing me endless ill."

But never has there been the strength in man
To move all heaven, putting it out of thought.
And so he must remember and look upward—
At nothingness all day; but evening brought
Dead stillness like a cannon at his heart:
The stillness of a battle timed to start.

Strain as he would to flee it, when the hour
Came suddenly with trumpets, he was waiting.
He looked, and they were there, and they were ready.
The toying time was over, and the baiting.
At last they were full weaponed, shaft and pike.
They were too cold and close now not to strike.

It seemed a woman's face and then a man's,
Swift-altering, swift-clearing; but the eyes
Changed never; they were fixed upon his trembling;
They stared beyond all pity and despise;
They waited without feeling, like the hands
Of judges when the nameless prisoner stands.

They waited, and he waited; then a voice
Broke heavily through stillness like a wave;
Far off, but heaving inland, and pursued
Uncountably by others, till the brave
High shore of his new courage shook and crumbled;
Then he was ready, then for all time was humbled.

"You will not be destroyed," he heard them saying—
Thickly rolled the waters, deep the waves;

"Nor comforted"—oh, hoarsely came their laughter;
"The final word is not the word that saves.
It is the merest verity, and men
Never may lose the sound of it again.

"This night will bring the end of us—the eyes—
And soon the hair you hated will be clouds
Parted with summer lightning; so our words,
Remembered, will resume their ancient shrouds,
Deep in the pit of time." But now they reared—
Armed waves of unrelenting war—and speared.

"We are the changeless person you denied.
We are the men and women you have slain.
Escaping after death, we wandered hither—
Home—and shall remain; and shall remain.
There is no such eternity for you.
The whole of you must perish as it grew:

"Quietly and palely, out of hearing,
With every dreadful gentleness confessed;
Nothing into nothing will go swiftly,
Passing us then whom you have not possessed.
We shall not know the moment, or inquire;
Forgetting you forever by this fire.

"The death of you is nothing, for you never
In all of time were implement to anguish.
We waited for the terror and the iron;
You softened them to love and let us languish.
Love? But it was feebleness and fear.
Pity? It was judgment and a sneer.

"We should have been invaded, as the sun
Drops suddenly, a serpent, into shade.
We needed to be threatened, as the knife
Flies—and there is blood along the blade.
There should have been an ambush and a foe,
With after-wounds, remembering that woe.

"There should have come against us in the dark
Hard hands, with sharp desire upon a cheek.
The eagle does no honor to the lamb
By kindness and the folding of his beak.
Our food was never danger: not a taste
Of fury, not a tempest hot with haste.

"These, these you must refuse us like a god.
You condescended to us, and we died:
Witnesses that you had been the savior—
Meek, meek! but swollen inwardly with pride.
Safe, safe—it was not worth the dying for.
We should have perished otherwise, by war.

"Or should, surviving battles all the way,
Have ripened to the center, and been warmed
By love that is the after-core of pain,
By pity that wounded wisdom has informed.
We should have lived or died—for it is one—
Full in the wind, full in the burning sun.

"For too much shadow, pale one, and excess
Of caring, we condemn you now to know:
The end of you, the all of you, is nothing.
Cold, cold the coming daylight and the snow.

Cold, cold! And so farewell, uncruel-kind,
Unborn, existless monster of the mind!"

When he could lift his face the sky was empty:
Soundless, like eternity, and white.
Dead white the falling dome; but where the ground was,
Greyness, as of ashes fresh and light.
But round his feet a darkness; and no day
Ever would burn the least of it away.

Tomorrow, and then always, it was round him,
A field of perfect darkness that he paced.
Not stumbling, for that wilderness is stoneless,
And over it hangs still the whitened waste.
No dawn or evening now beyond his eyes.
No alteration ever till he dies.

THE TOWER

Growing a Little Older

Growing a little older is suddenly
Standing a little still;
Then forward again, with something learned
Of the slow skill
Of skies,
Where motion dies.

Growing a little older is holding
One day a question back;
Then letting it go, with something seen
Of the faint crack
To crawl
Twixt nothing and all.

Growing a little older is hiding
Shivers of sudden fear;
Then letting them work, with something guessed
Of the deep spear
Of joy,
That too will destroy.

Why, Lord

Why, Lord, must something in us
  Yearly die?
And our most true remembrance of it
  Lie?
Until the pure forgetting
  By and by.

Why then must something other
  Come and grow?
Renewing us for nothing—save the
  Slow
Upbuilding of this bed
  Of needles, so.

Why is the soil not bitter
  Where we stand?
Whose, Lord, upon our roots
  The sweetening hand?
For so it is: we love
  No shallower land.

Joy Cannot Be Contained

Joy cannot be contained.
I know, for I have seen
The stricken eyes; and strained
To hear the blood's machine;

Have watched awhile and listened—
Terrible the stillness!
Then the eyes have glistened,
As from illness;

Then the heart has sounded,
Breaking in the dark;
As if the seas, impounded,
Had set again to work.

Fate Comes Unswerving

Fate comes unswerving like a frightened horse
Sky-maddened on a white mid-afternoon.
Fate comes unseeing, and the blinded hooves
Drum a shrill thunder to a noteless tune
That dies into the forest, where an owl
Returns it to the midnight and the moon.

Lean neither way, for nothing can escape.
No walker in a field knows whence it comes.
Only there is an instant when the dust
Whirls upward and the round horizon hums.
Then the feet loudest, and the final leap.
With afterward no dream of any drums.

Wit

Wit is the only wall
Between us and the dark.
Wit is perpetual daybreak
And skylark
Springing off the unshaken stone
Of man's blood and the mind's bone.

Wit is the only breath
That keeps our eyelids warm,
Facing the driven ice
Of an old storm
That blows as ever it has blown
Against imperishable stone.

Wit is the lighted house
Of our triumphant talk,
Where only weakly comes now
The slow walk
Of outer creatures past the stone,
Moving in a tongueless moan.

Praise

Praise is no crust of snow
That fell long since and formed,
And now one day will enter the shut earth—
Stale wine, and warmed.

Praise is directest rain
That comes when it is needed—
Cool in its newness, and descending where
Desire has seeded.

Praise is merest water—
Nothing, but enough.
Nor makes it any choice of how it feeds
Smooth ground or rough.

Praise falls on both alike,
And is at once beloved.
There is no good that is not prospered then;
Nor evil proved.

Pity

Pity is a naked sin,
  And a stripped weakness.
It does not wear the long clothes,
  The proud clothes of meekness.

Pity drops as suddenly,
  And is as frightening—
Entering the white breast—
  As streakéd lightning.

Pity comes, pity goes
  With a great rudeness,
Having not anything to do
  With love or goodness.

Meekness after Wrath

Of all perfected things,
Man-made or devil-god-made; yea, or both;
Nothing so undefective is, and fine,
As thundered wrath.

Nothing! save this mute
That follows like a lamb beside the udder,
Gesturing, when the mind—except it burst—
Cannot grow madder.

Nothing so pure as this:
The after-meekness, lacking any tongue;
Nor anything so powerful, though it lives,
Poor child, not long.

The Tower

The greater world is water,
The lesser world is land.
Out of moving vastness
Promontories stand.
Out of undulation
Heaves the firm sand.

The flood of moments, flowing,
Bears desire away;
Returning unto wideness
Distributable clay.
But not the hill of reason,
The mind's high play.

The greater world is water;
This little world is rock.
Beneath it subterranean
Sinews interlock;
And round it, silent, silent,
Wheels the invisible flock.

How Can Man His Stature Know

How can man his stature know,
  And so far grow?
How be incapable of less,
  Or of excess?
How can man the image find
That shall be matter to his mind?

How can man be like the least
  Clear herb or beast?
How be faithful, cold or warm,
  To his own form?
How can man as plainly be
As the sure mole, nor ask to see?

How can man contrive to borrow
  No more sorrow?
How return what he has taken?
  Nor be shaken,
When he wears the world no longer,
By the simplicity of hunger?

Never to Ask

Happy the mind alone,
Dissecting the body's mesh;
Happy, until the bone
Is there in a flash.
Happy this thing of knives
Until it arrives.

Better that it divide
Waves, and the ruly winds;
Let it go deep and wide
In the alien lands.
Let a plow quit the loam
When it comes home.

The moving whole, and the heat,
And the nine-day fever, love;
How the cracked heart can beat,
And eagle turn dove—
Let it be wisdom's task
Never to ask.

The Confinement

Whence, whence this heat of the brain?
I know, I know, he said—
The sleeplessness of continents and stars,
Rivers, and oily pavements, and old wars
Across too small a bed.

Whence, whence this fever-sight,
This still inflamed research?
I know. It is the press of the last sphere
To shrink its mighty pride and enter here—
All heaven in a church.

Whence, whence this burning bone,
This furnace in a skull?
Listen! I have heard the chafed complaint
Of thrice too large a cargo, hot and faint
Within too weak a hull.

Whence, whence this little fire
Whereon no fuel is put?
But it is fed with Africa's great groans,
And wrinkle-deep Aldebaran's live moans,
Recessed within a nut.

RETURN TO RITUAL

As from Arabian Ashes

As from Arabian ashes
A dustless bird arose;
And still the purple body
In a vast spiral goes,
  Envying the sun,
  The unrenewing one;

As from this waste of changes
There is a mind can fly,
And sail beyond confusion
In a fixed sky;
  But still it will remember
  Maytime and December;

So I, that now am starting,
And am so faithful-sworn,
Almost repent the voyage,
Almost am unreborn—
  Foreseeing, over the foam,
  The phoenix circling home.

Why Sing at All

Why sing at all, when the parched
Throat gives forth, unwillingly, dry sounds—
Wing-withered, that ascend
And rustle between the skull's deserted bounds?

The dim bone valleys there
Lie long and are unvisited by rain.
This dust, this music, rising,
Deepens the grey ground-cover, spreads the stain.

Why sing? But the tongue's attempt
May startle the chambered silence, and awake
Some spring whence joy, thin-flowing,
Trickles awhile; then rivers; and then a lake;

Then green, then sunny waters;
Then grass, and a bird-live forest moist with shade.
Why sing at all? But a sound
May serve, and a hopeless wasteland be unmade.

Oh the long, toneless drouth!
Oh the sunk pathways, shrivelled of their gladness!
Somehow the end arrives—
Drouth's end, with intermittency and madness.

Oh the sweet run of rain!
Oh the fresh floods, how carelessly they fall!
So will they have their end—
Yet sing! Or they will not come, not come at all.

Sing, and exceed this sound,
This shuffle of dust, this swish of particles blowing.
So will the vales be green,
And joy and desire stand up, and pride start growing.

Return to Ritual

The mother of life indulges all our wandering
Down the lone paths that narrow into peace.
She knows too well the gradual discovery
And the slow turning round until we cease—
Resolved upon the wide road once again
Whose dust hangs over day and mantles men.

Here is the drumming phalanx, here is the multitude;
Listen, and let us watch them over the stile.
We that remember clean moss ways and the tamaracks,
Let us be timorous now and shudder awhile.
We shall be early enough, no matter when,
Mother of dust, Oh mother of dust and men.

How time passes, here by the wall of eternity!
Even so soon we summon her; we are prepared.
Already these feet are lifting in a wild sympathy;
Who can remember the cool of a day unshared?
Mother of marches, mother, receive us then—
Listen! The dust is humming a song to the men.

Now This Joy

What was that life I led?
Answer, dumb wit that out of darkness clambers.
More yesterdays than now this joy remembers
Had I a liar's heart, pretending glad?

How could I think deception when the seated
Circle of old and young ones knew me wrong?
The multitude was hopeful of my tongue.
Was I the fool, and waited?

Was I the vain one, wanting
All a loud world to marvel upon my truth?
I do remember now, I heard them both—
My own still voice and that one, hoarsely chanting.

Was it too rough for rightness?
Answer, my new found wit, and bid me know
Every wild tune by night—without one flaw—
And whether I lose by lateness.

Another Music

The harmony of morning, and a thrush's
Throat among the sleep-deserted boughs;
Expiring mists that murmur all the day
Of a clear dusk, with music at the close;
Wind harp, rain song, night madrigal and round—
There is no word melodious as those.

Rage of the viol whose deep and shady room
Is sounded to a tempest by the strings;
Sweet keys depressed, swift rise upon a note
Whence all the narrow soul of music hangs;
The lifted flute, the reed, and horns agreeing—
Words in the wake of these are scrannel gongs.

In them another music, half of sound
And half of something taciturn between;
In them another ringing, not for ears,
Not loud; but in the chambers of a brain
Are bells that clap an answer when the words
Move orderly, with truth among the train.

It Is a Moveless Moment

It is a moveless moment, with no wings,
No feet to bring it flying. There it stays,
And there it would be always, like the dead,
But that we turn and find it on some days.
The merest turn; the neck would hardly know;
Then the sky dips, and all the landmarks go.

So is the world contracted to our eyes,
That, lacking any room for more, for less,
See all of it together, fine and small,
With no mark on it of our nothingness.
The littleness is lost that we could measure—
Knowing not then of this compacter treasure.

It is the moment when we understand,
Relaxing every effort to be wise.
It is the moment of our boundary's fall—
Proud stone, that we had armed against surprise.
It is the merest moment. Then again
We turn and are distinguishable men.

This Amber Sunstream

This amber sunstream, with an hour to live,
Flows carelessly, and does not save itself;
Nor recognizes any entered room—
This room; nor hears the clock upon a shelf,
Declaring the lone hour; for where it goes
All space in a great silence ever flows.

No living man may know it till this hour,
When the clear sunstream, thickening to amber,
Moves like a sea, and the sunk hulls of houses
Let it come slowly through, as divers clamber,
Feeling for gold. So now into this room
Peer the large eyes, unopen to their doom.

Another hour and nothing will be here.
Even upon themselves the eyes will close.
Nor will this bulk, withdrawing, die outdoors
In night, that from another silence flows.
No living man in any western room
But sits at amber sunset round a tomb.

On Such a Day as This One

On such a day as this one, time and sky
Flow round our shoulders mingled past division;
Past asking which, past hearing, for on high
One silence broods: the ultimate elision.

Such a day as this one lifts the seas
And loses them in air—as blue, as thin.
Yet not the seas; there is no current moving;
Not anything translucent, wave or fin.

Such a day as this one is the end;
Or would be if there were no shoulders listening.
Nothing but their question saves the world;
And that high sun, upon the silence glistening.

Phenomena

He thought some things were not to be compared.
They sprang from their own seed, that once had dared,
Dropping from several stars, to sow by night
One half of earth with unexplained delight.
Then morning came upon her equal feet,
And levelling her voice denied the sweet,
Sharp difference; she was not to be confused
By novelty of names, and form abused.
So noon and afternoon saw nothing strange.
Only at twilight did unreason range,
And only now by night is wisdom had
In a spun world of which the name is mad;
Only through darkness will the meaning shine
Of things that are but planets fallen fine;
Only the black meridian declares
That old descent from big and little Bears.

Laboratory Still Life

This apple now, and this smooth block of wood
That long ago forgot the watery tree
(The round red thing remembers in its wet heart,
The patient cube is mindless and immortal);
Set them on the table and declare
Their density, position, form, and mass.
Bring the slim brain that walks on calipers
(The little bow legs caper while you wait),
Bring the ruled retina, and pads of paper,
And take the sharpened pencil from its sheath.
Now weigh them well, the apple and the wood;
Let the mind's least antennae touch and write,
And writing, not remember what they touched.
There will be only figures at the finish,
Bodiless worms that if you stoop and peer
Cross-edgewise of the chart you will not find.
It is a flight of moths from skull to paper,
And back to the bone again, the hollow room.

Whereas the deep eye innocent of numbers
(Moist eye moving in a world of shapes,
Warm eye wonderful in child or man)
Sees only a bright apple and a cube.
The deep eye looks, and there is nothing more
Than a red apple with a watery heart,
Than a blank face of wood that has forgotten.
The deep eye looks, and not a word comes forth.
Nothing is here for counting or dividing,
Nothing to understand; nothing to add.
Only the red round face grows redder, rounder,
And the six flattened cheeks widen a little,
Complacent of their enduringness indoors.

Time and Water

The humped back of the beaver, and the four
Curved teeth that bring the poplar splashing down—
There in the lake it lies, and the silver branches
Turn, in the day, in the night, to a watery brown—
The upthrust and pond-dividing whiskers
Say that the world is wet, and seasons drown.

Swimming in darkness, nearing his willow dam,
Pausing before he climbs to the dripping sticks,
He is eternally far from hills and deserts,
Roads, and the odorous barns, and the drying ricks;
The beaver is only credulous of meadows
A rising river enters and moistly licks.

Diving in darkness, down to the lily roots,
Turning and paddling off and rising slow,
The beaver descends again and finds his burrow,
Rises again and is home, and he says: I know.
Water is endless, time is an undulation,
Water is all there is, and seasons flow.

Spread, Spread

Spread, spread, November rain;
Sleep-bringing river, widen so
That every meadow takes the stain
Of rising death's first overflow.

Instruct the trees that are adorned
Too bravely now, and drown their blood.
Leave not a sunwise slope unwarned
Against the white, the final flood.

Invisibly the banks of time
Give way; the unseen river reaches.
The mist of change begins to climb
And slide along the grassy beaches,

Sliding until no further drop
Of dryness lives in any vein;
When even change will, flowing, stop,
And rocks no more remember rain.

Till then, November, spread your brown
Foretelling waters like a tide;
That, when the silence deepens down,
Even slumber will have died.

The Other House

The leafless road midwinters by itself,
And the slat gate, wired open, never swings.
Should the loop rust, and weaken in the wind,
Two posts will join that now are separate things;
Forgetful how they guarded the little space
One entering coat could fill, one entering face.

We spoke of strangers happening to pass,
And wondered if such openness were wise.
But the posts know; they have not felt each other
Since the high sun was shaded from their eyes.
We spoke of footprints; but a sparrow's track
Is all that diverges in and circles back.

Even a look from us so distant here,
Even a sigh might leave its line on snow:
Up the still road and in, then round and round;
Then stopping, for we must no further go.
Let the line pause mid-yard; there let it end,
Lest the sad chimneys smile, and smoke pretend.

She Is the Youngest

She is the youngest of the wood,
Yet is there many a newer thing.
The hemlock with the ragged hood
Droops in everlasting spring.

Above the snow, or when the leaves
Lie well around her, safe and dead,
Not a wind but lowly weaves
The delicate spine; deflects the head;

Picks up the green and greyish cape
That all but flowed into the earth.
Grave, grave the maiden shape,
Out of love awhile with mirth.

Sad, sad, but it is well:
How she looks upon the ground
Cures the melancholy spell
Of age and coldness all around.

Sad, sad, but what she means
Is that the world is old and strong;
Indulgent still to one that leans
On youthful sorrow overlong.

Somewhat More Slowly

Somewhat more slowly, lengthener of days—
O, you that pull the crusted nails of winter—
Somewhat more slowly work. Within is lying
One who would not hear too soon the splinter
Of wrapping-boards; nor see too soon your light
Enter and like a thief put out the night.

Lay down your hammer somewhere in the snow,
Deep snow and dark, and drop your chisel after.
Sleep there upon the wind, as far away
As April, and be deaf to this my laughter—
Muffled in the linen of a box
Upon whose lid Time comes, Time comes and knocks.

But comes not yet if you lie long and dream,
And, wakened on a morning, doubt your eyes.
Look then for those you lost—you will upturn them,
Cold beneath the snow—and slowly rise,
And slowly make approach. I shall be rested;
Nor is death then unwillingly molested.

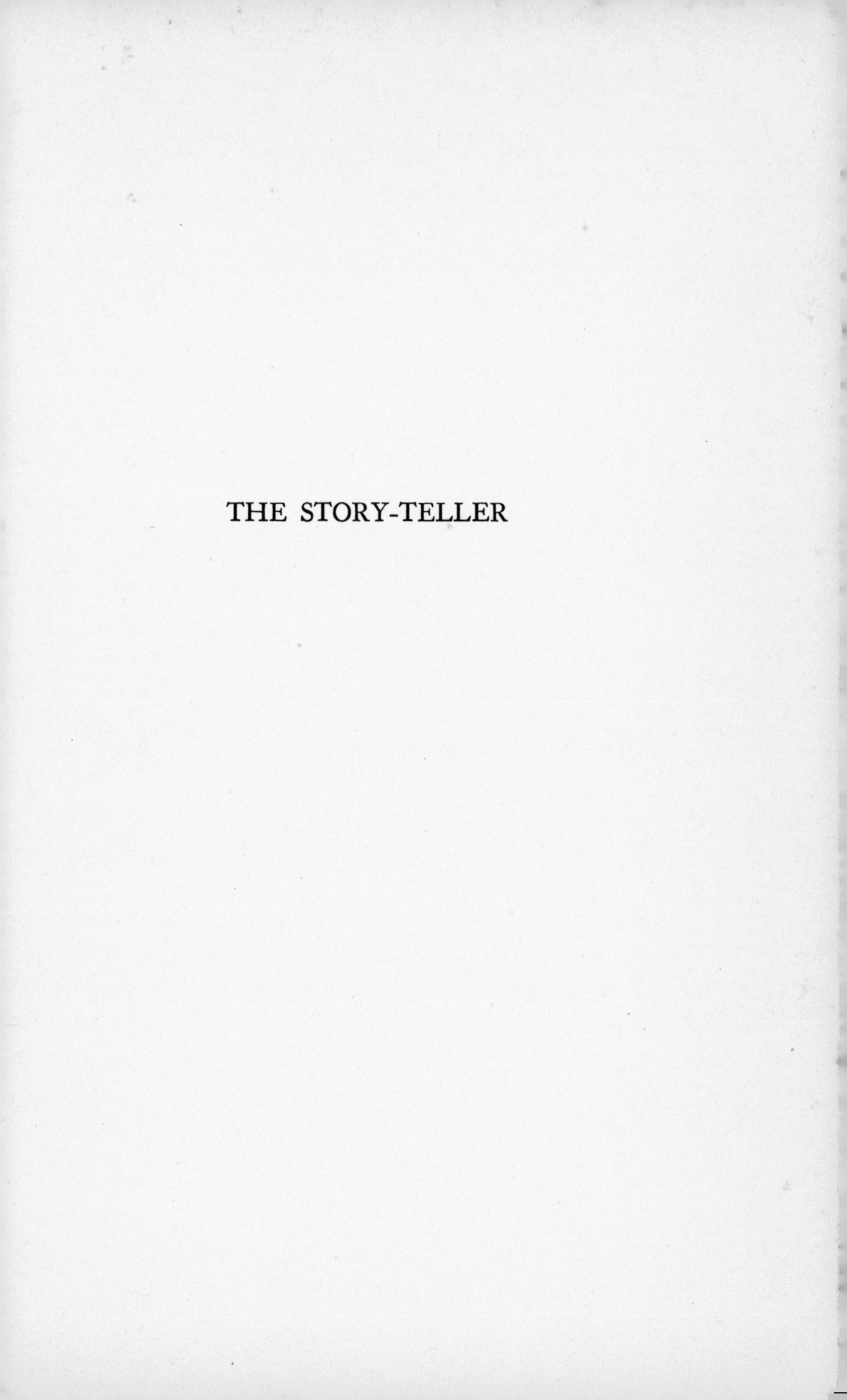

THE STORY-TELLER

What Is the Hour

What is the hour, how loud the clock,
When the heart knows itself for rock?
Or is it ignorant? Does the rose
More silently than centuries close?
Perhaps no man so long ahead
Predicts the flint, proclaims the dead.

There was the year it opened wide
And tore a hole in his calm side.
Strange the petals' hingéd strength,
Staining, staining all his length
With wasted blood; until they shut,
And he forgot the flesh's cut.

There was the day it stirred again
And straightway stopped; and chilled him then.
There was the fear his pain had ceased.
But it returned, and it increased;
There was a rose within him said
He must be happy while it bled.

Is there no rose inside him now?
Is there no vein to disavow
This rocky stillness? So he stands,
Exploring silence with his hands;
Wonders, waits; and leans to hear
That valvéd sound of yesteryear.

He Was Not Wise

He was not wise to dally with the curves
Of earth and set his fancy continent-free.
The game at first was merry, and he smiled;
He was at home with aliens, land and sea—
Stoking a fire with bullies west by south
In the same hour that Persia curled her mouth.

He felt the flame, he tapped the pearly teeth;
He blessed himself and nestled to his kind.
But then he scudded further, and beheld
Tall men of China chatting as they dined;
Flew on, and by an island strange of name
Struck sail; for now the terror of it came.

One porch too many, folding in its shade
Some brow unseen, some lip, destroyed the count.
Here was the death of number, the abstract
Mute reckoning—how dim the pure amount!
How far desire, how close the little space
Encircling every watched and silent face.

The Escape

Going from us at last,
He gave himself forever
Unto the mudded nest,
Unto the dog and the beaver.

Sick of the way we stood,
He pondered upon flying,
Or envied the triple thud
Of horses' hooves; whose neighing

Came to him sweeter than talk,
Whereof he too was tired.
No silences now he broke,
No emptiness he explored.

Going from us, he never
Sent one syllable home.
We called him wild; but the plover
Watched him, and was tame.

The Hermit

On a grey hill above the talk of streams,
Where not a risen rock repeats the wind
And no tree groans with standing, and no grass
Rustles upon itself, the still feet stay.

Here no hidden deity, bespoken,
Utters a thunderous answer ill or good.
Only the feet are here, and these straight hands,
And one pale mind, sending its column up

Of silence. It is silence that he says
Will wash the earth below him of its pain.
Words are but fire we pour into old wounds
That long ago wove blood into the sky.

So the white column, rising, spreads and comes
Down softly midst our sounds, and we are soothed.
He says the sky is healing, too; and hears
Some day the whole world dreaming under snow.

Memorial

If nothing else, let this poor paper say—
Outwhitening time and those subduing voices—
How once a black-eyed doctor drove away,
After she died, behind his dappled horses.

This shall not be memorial for her,
Nor him, the black-eyed man, nor for the dappled
Shadow upon two breasts; but as they were
That morning, let each word of them be tripled.

Within a room she lay, and they were going—
The bright defeated man and those long faces
Slanted upon the wind—and time was snowing
Forgetfulness already, as he uses.

And still he would, had not this paper power,
Holding the four together, to remember.
These hungry hooves will not outstep the hour,
Nor the dark eyes come ever home to slumber.

Going Home

His thought of it was like a button pressed.
Far away the figures started going;
A silver watch ticked in a sleepy vest,
And on the porch an apron string was blowing.

His thought again was like a fly-wheel cranked,
And circular machinery set gliding.
The little town turned truly, as the banked
Brown houses followed in and out of hiding.

His travel, once he went, was like the troop
Of farmers in an autumn to the fair.
All year the field was flat, but now the coop
Of turkeys and the horses would be there;

People moving everywhere and nodding,
Little boys with birds and yellow whips;
A person at a counter would be wadding
Rifles, and the girls would hold their hips.

His coming near was like the soft arrival
Of gods around a thing that they have made;
And will again forget; but long survival
Saves it, once again the trance is laid.

Highway Ghost

The gravelly road is gone.
Old people, whirled behind a windy wheel,
Huddle their coats about them and remember
How they went proudly once;

How the eight ringing feet
Flung gritty pebbles into the grass,
And how the four high iron tires
Sang in the sand.

Old men, silently borne
Where now the way goes black and wide
And smoothly like a river into the wood,
Old men, saying nothing,

See a white horse come curving,
Swinging an empty buggy round the hill.
The white feet fall without a noise, approaching,
And thin wheels lightly follow.

Spokes flicker by,
And grey heads, nodding at each other, turn
To see between the curtains what is there.
Nothing at all is there.

The gravelly road is gone,
And dim eyes, drawn around a bend forever,
Have in them only history, and the fall
Of a slow shadow.

Old Tune

The words of this old woeful song
Float so merrily along,
Out of ages that they sweeten
Though the hearts of men were eaten.
This old tale of souls that brake
Falls softly on us, flake by flake.

He raised the knife;
She spread her gown
And begged for life;
But only a frown
Got ever that wife;
Got ever that wife,
Hey derrikin down.

This tune that came so long a road
Has shed the sorrow of its load.
Though its burden will endure
The air is merciful and pure.
This bitter tale of one that died
Leaves only honey in our side.

The knife it fell;
She spread her coat
And made a well
Of that white throat.
She made a well
For him in hell,
High dollikin dote.
So merrily float
With him in hell,
High dollikin dote.

The Story-Teller

He talked, and as he talked
Wallpaper came alive;
Suddenly ghosts walked,
And four doors were five;

Calendars ran backward,
And maps had mouths;
Ships went tackward
In a great drowse;

Trains climbed trees,
And soon dripped down
Like honey of bees
On the cold brick town.

He had wakened a worm
In the world's brain,
And nothing stood firm
Until day again.

Recognition Scene

From many a mile the son,
From a third of the earth the father;
Each of them bearing his sign
Of kinship high as a feather.
Dusky the hour, and late;
What shall we do that wait?

We shall not quit the grove,
We shall not rise and scatter.
Something deep as the grave
Holds every heart in a flutter.
Dewy the night. No bird—
There! Who trembled? Who heard?

Who spied him, tall in the west?
Old is the night, and bitter.
Far in the eastern waste
Who caught a faint hoof and a clatter?
Now closer—now here—he draws—
Oh, insupportable pause!

To a Friend Hesitating before Change

Shatter the moldy glass
Wherein you look too long.
The arm of time is ready,
And trembles at the gong.
Nod and let it fall,
And stand outside the wall.

Such suddenness of sound
Will loosen every tree,
And though your house is broken
The mountains will run free
With frosty colors, new and fine,
Set upon each curvéd line.

Or else—and who can say?—
Darkness will be there,
With danger at its heart,
And teeth about to tear.
Even then I tell you change.
Anything, so it be strange.

Dumb Beast, Regret

Dumb beast, regret;
Dumb beast, so ever-hungry and so sly;
Listen where you are sitting—in what cave
I know not, but the path is foul and wry;
Listen; I am begging of you yet:
Although you starve, forget.

Cool, slippery paws;
You more than four sleek feet that know my way;
Be this one night confounded; let the mist
Confuse you at the turnings until day,
When though the jaws you bring be lean and dying,
Turn back upon their crying.

Keep home, regret;
Dumb eyes, that know my heart's dark flesh so well,
Be closed in utter shadow, and dream on
Of bloodless feasts that no one lives to tell.
Haunt sepulchres, haunt sleepers in the sea;
But now not me, not me.

The Friendship

It was so mild a thing to see,
People saw it silently.
Such peace was in it people said
It would not alter with them dead.

None knew the difficult design
They worked to follow, line by line,
Nor in the sending of a glance
How much was art, how little chance;

Nor how that courtesy was kept
Wherethrough no step was overstepped.
There was no harshness in these hands
That wove a set of silken bands—

Binding honor unto praise,
And tying tenderness, that lays
No single burden on a friend
As far as to the tethered end.

Not a disagreeing word
Between the two was ever heard.
But when it ended with them dead,
Buried bones got up and bled.

The Bystanders

Who is this host of folk this fair spread day?
And who these few that stand and do not run—
Watching the others only, in the way
Of the dark stars outside the circled sun?
Strange, but the less are greater; only they
Have number; here the many are the one.

Strange, but the host is single, like a beam
Of noon that folds its particles inside.
Strange, but the few are many. Yet they dream
Of darkness, and of standing unespied,
Watching the rabble current—envied stream!
One river! though it is both deep and wide.

Here on the shore, in an imagined night,
They stand and wrap their arms; but on each face
Falls the dead flush of a reflected light
That fringes their aloofness as with lace—
The memory of a multitude's sweet might;
The flowing, and the union, and the grace.

The greyness all around them is old mist
Engendered by the chill of their contempt.
These were the few that labored to resist,
And the flood set them, separate and exempt,
Here on the windless shore—but now they twist
With a new longing, and the frail attempt,

Returning, to go smoothly once again
Down the sole river where the lashes close
And the eyes, sinking, dream of dancing men.
Yet here they stand in their uneven rows,
Superior forever—until when
Death lifts a hollow socket-bone and blows.

The Unwanted Lonely

Make way for them, who nothing see
Beyond the shadow of their eyes.
Make way for that—the sharpened cone
That shoots before them now as flies
The pointing night of an eclipse,
Wherein a day's triangle dies.

Make way for them; they lost their hope
Longer ago than faith can heal.
They walk condemned—yet think to find
Some face perhaps that still can feel.
But let them pass you; be not one
Transfixéd willingly with steel.

Make way for them, and turn your head
Perhaps with pity; yet be strong.
What they can penetrate you with
Is thin and poor; but it is long,
And will not break. It is the fear
Of light's dislike; and is not wrong.

The Talkers to Themselves

They are little rodents
   Whistling in a wall;
But every stone is glass there,
And we can see them all
   Building their own dark
   With mumble and remark.

With little pointed elbows
   They threaten the great night;
But there is not a shadow yet,
And we can watch the flight
   Of little frantic fears
   About their closing ears.

Every little warrior
   Trembles there alone,
Behind a harmless breastwork
Of never heeded moan;
   And what he sometimes says
   In stunted sentences.

Laugh Not Too Loudly

He said that we must thank the gods
For vanity, which like a wheel
Whirls a man or woman now and then
Till the soul bulges, and a giddy heel
Is pivotal to something oversized.
He said the vain were vases under seal.

"Opened, though, there's nothing there."
Admitting this, he only smiled.
"As barren, top and bottom, as a tomb—
Not even filled with future, like a child."
He said this too was true; but must insist
That vacancy not always be reviled.

"They are the sacrifice," he said,
"So that a miracle can be.
The soul, that is invisible, becomes
A something then which anyone may see.
Laugh not too loudly, for the gods translate
Only the brave, the wild. The rest go free."

The Philanderer

It was the very innocence of love;
Though words were whispered that have toppled walls
And taken sleeping lives, he was a dove
Nesting in little gables, whither his calls
Brought momentary mates to share the dim,
Sweet dawn along the eaves, and strut with him.

The nearness of the morning was what saved him.
He never would have dared the naked night;
And they were such as never would have braved him
In the true dark. It was a pretty fright,
A flutter of alarm beside a door;
Then the sun came, and there was nothing more.

It was delicious doom to be suspended
Thus between having and not having them.
What never had begun was never ended,
Save that some tried a deeper stratagem
And flew to him at midnight. Then he ran,
Lest now he be possessed as proper man.

He ran, and they were glad that it was so.
It was their doom to play at the surrender.
Having themselves again, they still could go
Remembering the eyes of this pretender;
Leaving a lonely portion of them there,
Under the soft eaves beyond the stair.

Antipathies

Item, the man by whom he was reminded
Of the dead calfish days before the rope
Broke, and he ran till he was tired of running;
This fellow, staring here and snorting hope,
Dangled the ancient tether past a wall.
Right there it was. Had he come thence at all?

Item, another one who knew too well
The paths that he had come by, if he came;
Who shrank the middle distance till it sat,
A small divided desert, full of tame
Four-footed memories, that by day remarked
His face with little coyote eyes and barked.

Item, the newly known one with the brow
That wore a different wisdom from his own.
What loss in that, he wondered? Yet he saw
How each comes only once, and comes alone;
And asked the wind if many wandered off
In a sheep's night, missing the wether's cough.

Modern Sinner

He was of an old mind,
And so would have preferred
Consciences less kind
Around him when he erred:
Darker wires to bind
The scarcely cagéd bird.

Such wings as now he wore
Were lifted quite in vain
Without a narrow door
To take them in again,
And shut, and hide the sore
No probing would explain.

For still he could be healed
And try another flight.
Now all was sunny field,
With never a stroke of night.
So wearily he wheeled
Into the endless white.

The Bore

He was not helped by knowing well
How cold he made us, and how weary.
He must have told himself at last
He was not saved by being sorry.

Better than anyone he saw
The stealthy turn, the trained escape,
Or if he came too soon for these,
How frantic courtesy could wrap

Desire to fly with skill to stay—
A twitching wing beneath the feather;
How within a greying eye
The kindest agony can gather.

And did he witness this too well?
Was then the knowledge but the cause?
Long time we looked, but could not find
A way of learning why he was.

Partitions

She fled into herself before the sun.
When the wind rose her thoughts became a thicket,
Drawing her in, while softly one by one
The leaves would search her wound and weep and lick it.
None of our voices ever got so far
As to the trembling center of that maze.
We found the margin easy, but a bar
Of shadows lay across the deeper ways.
Sometimes we waited; then a face would peer
Half woman through the laurel, and half deer.

She was afraid of openness and act.
A deed would tear the bravest barrier down.
She loved the lone partitions where she tracked
Green fancies never trampled into brown.
We called to her, extending our warm hands;
She only stared and smiled, and we could see
No meaning in that brow, or in the bands
Of fear that tightened, tightened quietly.
Safe in her lanes she wandered. Was she wise?
The answer is dead leaves upon the eyes.

The Photographs

The person on the sidewalk is possessed
Of a loud secret, capable of crying.
This haster among the many holds himself
Like a mute man that presently is dying.
And yet there is old age for him—and those
In the pressed parcel he would be untying.

His children's faces, wrapped against the sun,
Sing low between the still sleeve and the heart.
This holder of his tongue sends more than breath
Invisibly ahead of him—sends part,
Sends all of him, advancing as he goes
To a frail music, soundless at the start.

He hears it there and hardly may contain
His joy that Time can sing so young a song.
He follows it, prophetical of days
When the grown burden suddenly is strong.
Thereafter—but his smiling is confined
To the live moment, mercifully long.

It Should Be Easy

It should be easy, letting the small feet go;
Quick should it turn, the necessary knob;
Empty this porch of any following eye
Fixed upon waves wherein a head shall bob—
Now up, now down forever; but it rises,
And floats and disappears among the mob.

We should be sure the shoulders will return,
And the hands reach and click the lock again.
We should be thoughtless, occupying days
With a new ritual modified to men.
We should be proud and let a trumpet say
How close the waters welter about the den.

And solitude would soothe us, were it not
For the slow sound of breakers near the door:
Reminders of the many farther out,
Of the lost many, nameless evermore,
That young with pride set seaward long ago,
Leaving the grey alone, the mother shore.

It would be easy, letting the cap depart,
And the small face that never looks around;
But the firm coast line—suddenly it bends;
Suddenly it follows, and the sound
Of hopeless cries is heard; until the waves
Wash once again on straight and silent ground.

The Monument

Swift cruelties to children are a pyramid
Built of soft stones that harden under time.
They were not quarried, they were not shapened craftily,
They were unconscious then of granite or lime.
They were not planned at all. But they have altitude;
They are too high for memory to climb.

When memory is merciless, and labors,
Gaining the topmost cube, and lingers there,
The view is of an undivided wasteland
Down from the breather's height through darkened air;
Nothing familiar now except the still voice
Bidding him measure deserts if he dare.

Better the climb untaken, and the guilt
Forgotten, could the mind go clear around.
But the long way is endless, and the stones
Are numberless; immovable the mound.
It is our own memorial, and stands
In front of us wherever we are bound.

Simple Beast

With rope, knife, gun, brass knucks, and bloody laws
Earth everywhere is noisy—not with paws
Of leopards silent, not with saber-toothed
Long tigers paced all year upon and smoothed.
That was the age of hunger, when the taken
Fourfoot with a moment's dread was shaken;
Then the slow-closing eyes; then over stones
Time's scattering of the picked, the cleanly bones.
This is the age of anger, when the hail
Beats corn and rose alike, and leaves a trail
More sluttish that it tells man's appetite.
This is the age of gluttony and spite.
With lash and bomb, blue fire and bayonet
Earth everywhere is littered. Earth is wet
With blood not drained for drinking, earth is loud
With sounds not made for hearing, earth is plowed
By steel that will not reap it. Earth is least
Like what earth was when beast was simple beast.

Strike Then the Rusted Strings

Strike then the rusted strings.
Pound, pound the sluggard voice.
And bid deposéd kings
With our poor selves rejoice.

Hang branches from the rafters;
But where the doors have been,
Hang thorns to prick the laughter
Of lost ones coming in.

Pour liquor that will widen
The skull's already smile.
The darkness we have died in,
Let it be red awhile.

Let it be white, and burn us
Unto the finest ash.
Let music be the furnace.
Let every fiddle flash.

Ha! and now we gather.
Ho! and now we part.
Let every bone be lather,
Next to the fiery heart.

Let every arm, upswinging,
Be melted as it goes.
So, to such a singing,
The stoniest sadness flows.

Be still! for they are letting
The last poor devil in.
Now shut the door! forgetting
Whatever deaths have been.

Ha! and now we gather.
Ho! and now we part.
(The last one dances rather
Stiffly at the start.)

Epitaphs

For Two Men

When these were idle shouting boys
Their mouths could make an equal noise.

When these were young and earnest men
One managed all the talking then.

When he grew famous he forgot
The other one that here doth rot.

But which is now the louder dust
The eyeless worms have not discussed.

For One Unburied

Stranger, do not think to find
The banter here of parting bones;
We let the desert wind unbind
His flesh, and scatter it like stones.

He was impatient with the jest
Of eyes enlarging underground.
So his are open to the west,
And day diminishing around.

There all the pieces of him lie,
Too far apart to understand
The comedy of ribs awry
And sockets filling up with sand.

For a Maiden

This girl was not to go
Until two shoulders cast
Shadow upon her snow,
And melted it at last.

The warmth she had within
Still waited to be found.
The coverlet is thin.
Be curious, cold ground.

Exploring with your frost,
Go down as deep, as deep,
As linen; then be lost
In thaw, and a long sleep.

For a Fickle Man

Two women had these words engraved—
The first and last of whom he tired.
One told the other, while they lived,
The thing between them he desired.

What now it is they do not know,
Or where he seeks it round the sun.
They only ask the wind to blow,
And that his will be ever done.

For a Jester

The things he used to do, and laugh,
Are blown along with other chaff.

Never to rustle and arise,
Here the kernel of him lies,

The solid portion of the man.
And this we count—but feel the fan,

And lift a sudden far-off look
At what the wind of harvest took.

For Two Brothers

Let no man say that either mind
Heard willingly the scythe behind.

The edge was on them ere they knew,
With that undone which words could do—

And now is done upon a stone
That time has not come back and mown.

Until it tumbles, brother and brother
Understand they loved each other.

REPORT OF ANGELS

There Is No Language

There is no language that the heart learns wholly.
One thing it fails at, though it deeply tries.
It cannot ask a question; it is only
Skilful in surrenders and replies.

Most eagerly it answers, and most softly
It gives the needy asker surest proof.
But when itself is doubtful comes the dumbness.
What most is meant remains the most aloof.

The heart is never childlike, though it stammers,
And half the words it weeps for are refused.
The ancient one can do no more than answer;
It cannot beg, as once the young one used.

Cool-Throated Hound

Cool-throated hound, deep-voiced and most exact,
Most cleanly in delight, most clear in hunger,
Live, live, that in the end I shall have lacked
Nothing, having you, eternal stranger.

My lithe musician, leaning on the wind,
Harmonious of iron and melancholy,
Lead, lead, that every forest shall be dinned
With prophecies of me resounding truly.

Hound, hound of my desire, no matter where,
Keep running; I am here and I will follow.
Be, be, that I may be, and up the air
Scent always Joy, with Love, his deathless fellow.

Report of Angels

"Nothing for envy there"—
Folding their dustless wings—
"Nothing, beyond this pair
Of impossible things:

"Love, wherein their limbs,
Trembling, desire to die;
And sleep, that darkly swims,
Drowning each brain and eye.

"Nothing is there for us,
Who may not cease to know;
But heaven was merciless,
Fixing our eyelids so;

"Whereon no tide may run,
Rolling its night ahead;
Where love is a labor done,
And death long since was dead."

Always Evening

You eyes, forever west of afternoon,
And oh, you setting-sun-descended hair,
Make every day of absence die more soon
Than minutes, that it may be evening there
Forever, shadeless eyes,
Wherein all distance dies.

Forever be the hour that is the end,
The hour that blackens daytime and the grass,
O eyes, it is the moment when you send
Hither most heat, as through a burning-glass;
Hither excessive light,
Love's lie against the night.

Be always spicy evening, my love's mind,
Contracting to yourself the deaths of roses.
Gather into an instant every kind
Of fragrance that the waste of time encloses,
Letting the long world shrink
Into one drop; and drink.

His Lady Lacks Not Anything

His lady lacks not anything
Save a beholder:
Wiser born than was the king,
Yet noway older;
Young and wise, and fit to sing
What none has told her.

Say it quickly to the queen:
How she dissembles,
Letting only that be seen
Which time resembles;
How at the rest, the ageless green—
How my verse trembles.

Tell her nevertheless I know;
And am suspended
Here between an ancient woe
And one unended.
Music fails, as long ago;
Nor can be mended.

They Were Good Fortune's

They were good fortune's maid and man;
The gift of love between them passed
As lightly as the snow comes,
And silent to the last.

They talked, but not of what was given;
There it hung, by chance descended;
Each but held a hand out,
And exchange was ended.

So colorless, so soft a thing,
So free—they would not name it love;
It was but whitened wind-fall,
Slanting from above.

So painless, it was not themselves. . . .
They never knew that flesh can tear,
Suddenly, as boughs break
Upon snow-heavy air.

The Willingness

The willingness that Lucy wears
Becomes her like a fitted gown;
Nor is there any seam to see
Until the thing is down—
The whole of it, as if a lone
Young tree had cast its crown.

Those leaves that make so loose a ring
Will never again be hung together.
The flying bird does not regain
A single drifted feather.
So Lucy stands forever now
Unlaced against the weather.

The willingness that Lucy wore
Was nothing to this naked side.
And yet the truth of her is both;
The raiment never lied.
Desire without, desire within—
So is love simplified.

The First Blow

Embrace it, though it be
A salt new inland sea;
Make the most of such a pain
As never now can come again.

It is the first, and quenches
Even what it drenches;
Heart, too soon you will outgrow
This unremembered overflow.

You will grow wise, and lose
Black honey from a bruise;
Anticipate this weeping while
The drained, inevitable smile.

Let Not Your Strictness Vary

Let not your strictness vary;
Be less, be less than just;
In a mild January
We miss the frost.

I have a store of wood in;
The windows well are stopped;
I sleep a sleep that sudden
August would interrupt.

Let not your coldness, going,
Leave too well prepared
One whom years of snowing
Have into virtue snared.

Let every May-fly slumber,
And in deep holes the fox.
Nor will I lie and number
Centuries to equinox.

The Difference

Day after day, for her, the sun
Drew semicircles smooth and high.
A week was seven domes across a desert,
And any afternoon took long to die—
Rounding the great curve downward not too fast,
Not falling; not a shadow ran awry.

His day was two thin lightning lines
Pitched here one instant like a tent;
Then night; and there was neither afternoon
Nor evening to be witness how they went.
His day was but a burning at the top;
Then the steep fall, and every spark was spent.

They lived together only thus:
One tick of noon their common day;
And many a noon, so meeting, each would ask:
What found the other past the middle way?
But neither he whose leap was like a star
Nor she who curved and swung could ever say.

She Said Too Little

She said too little, he too much.
She drooped; he could not droop enough.
Between a sigh, between a song,
Simplicity defeated both.

He was importunate with proof,
But undervalued then the pause.
She was judge of something else,
Something silent in the blood,

Something destined to be loud
If only words could fail and wait.
She never heard it; or explained
What sound is deeper than the throat.

They were not different save in this:
He paused too little, she too long.
But each was farther at the close
Than all northwest, and spreading storms.

First Alarm

Nothing could be stranger
Than this silence was.
There never had been danger
Until the sharpened saws
Of pride cut in and in,
Unbuilding what had been.

Nothing was the matter,
Except they barely talked.
The end had come of chatter.
They whipped it, but it balked
At climbing the two hills
Of their awakened wills.

There was a time, perhaps,
When they would do with stillness;
But now it seemed relapse
Into a worse illness
Than any mending lover
Ever got up and over.

Let There Be No More Talk

Let there be no more talk
Till this new love can walk.
When he is grown a manly child
There may be many words, and wild.
There may be silences as sore
As he was murdered with, and more.
Now he is born again,
Let us remember then.

Nor warn him as we pass,
This weanling of the grass.
He still is ignorant of the snow
Through which his naked heels must go.
Let him learn, and disappear
Down many a road for many a year.
Though it be overlong,
Then is he old and strong.

I Passed the Sleepy Ridges

I passed the sleepy ridges
Whereon my love had looked.
Her house was by the bridges
Where the slow rivers crooked.

Many and many a morning,
As the white sun would rise,
The darkness, at her warning,
Flowed down upon her eyes,

That took it in and saved it;
Oh! there was room and more.
With her own tears she laved it,
There by the turning shore.

There were two crooked streams there.
Heavily went they round.
Now darkness only seems there,
And dewless is the ground.

Her house was by the bridges;
But now all three are gone.
I recognized the ridges;
Paused, and travelled on.

By Their Own Ignorance

By their own ignorance I knew them,
And the tall way they stood;
Denying she had ever wandered through them,
Entering that wood.

By their indifference I proved them,
Those high old border trees;
Pretending that no thunderbolt had grooved them—
Each heart at ease.

No lesser lie could they be brooding:
A footfall had not died.
The truth, I said, was weaker praise; intruding
No more upon that pride.

Will I Weep Then

Will I weep then, secret master,
For the word not spoken faster?
Will I weep that had the choosing
Of all time, and spent it musing?
Will I weep that felt love's air
Like an embrace, and did but stare?

Or will I, master, count me wise
Because I watched the moth-wing rise;
Observed the trembling of the sun
Upon each vein, and so did run;
But always since remember well
How love rose on, and never fell?

HERE THEN HE LAY

Here Then He Lay

In Memoriam
C.L.V.D.
1857–1933

Where mild men gathered he was half at home,
Though all of him was treasured for his eyes.
The other half, dark-ranging, never paused;
And still it goes, and still the curving skies
Contain the soundless footfalls of a man
Whose moving part our obsequies outran.

Here then he lay, and stationary flowers
Were like the words of good men come to see:
All pure, all nodding whiteness; final proof
Of wonder—save the last, the far degree.
Already, while the compliments uncurled,
He gathered with the dark ones of the world;

Came noiseless up, and shed the afternoon
Like a thin shoe behind him; so he stands
Eternally in twilight, and the rest
Acknowledge nothing alien in his hands,
That hour by hour acknowledge nothing there
Save the full dusk and the sufficient air.

It was the eyes that brought him; so he stays
Despite the something different in his walk.
Round, round he moves among them, and each one
Is different—more the panther, more the hawk,

More the slow-treading dove; yet no disguise
May alter their unburiable eyes.

Both sun and shade are in them, pair by pair,
Both everlasting day and boundless dark.
This is the field to which the few have come;
These are the visions death could never mark.
There was no way to deepen such a gaze
Save with this dusk, abstracted from all days.

There now his feet fall silently, and now
He is both old and young—his hope the same;
Ranging the mild world, sowing it with pride,
And leaving not a meadow of it tame;
Praising all men that have the quenchless eye;
Yet loving the unlustred who will die.

There was a pride within him that refused,
As the sun does, to scorn the lesser thing;
And there was winter wildness, blowing up
The smallest out-of-mind leaf-underling,
That, looked upon, came quick to life; but then
With his warm night he covered it again.

We praised him for the kindness of his talk,
And a meek heart mortality had kissed.
We might have sung the justice of a glance
Wherein not even littleness was missed.
Then, then we should have added his desire
For the great few and the unburning fire.

We told a tale of charity, and hands
Long practiced in the banishment of pain.

We knew his mind's ambition, and his tongue's
Swift temper, and his wisdom to refrain.
We should have known how nothing held him back
From the great dusk and from the trodden track.

He treads it now, and he is never tired.
There where he goes, intensity is ease.
No strict requirement but of old was met;
The world at last is single that he sees.
All one, the world is round him that he saw
When he looked past us, innocent of awe.